SAILING TIPS

SAILING TIPS

1000 NEW WAYS TO SOLVE OLD PROBLEMS

WILLIAM M. BURR, JR.

ST. MARTIN'S PRESS
NEW YORK

Of the more than 1000 hints in this book, many are passed along as firsthand information; others are based on accumulated lore and have been used by other sailors. The author and the publisher recommend that you use both care and common sense when applying any of the suggestions in this book.

Design by Jaye Zimet

Library of Congress Cataloging-in-Publication Data

Burr, William M.
    Sailing tips: 1000 new ways to solve old problems / William M. Burr, Jr.
      p. cm.
    ISBN 0-312-02977-2
    1. Sailing. I. Title.
GV811.B88 1989
797.1'24—dc 19   89-30093
                                                                              CIP

First Edition
10 9 8 7 6 5 4 3 2 1

To my son, Alexander, who cheerfully endured much of the summer of 1988 with a father who was continually busy with the book.

And to my wife Natasha, who spent uncounted hours counseling and editing. Without her unfailing help, this book would not have been written.

CONTENTS

FOREWORD

Sailors can spend a lifetime learning the art of tuning and tackling difficult problems. The most powerful forces on earth are the wind and the sea. These forces combined with the harsh effects of saltwater can cause every imaginable problem on yachts. Fixing broken equipment, dealing with harsh weather, and anticipating maintenance problems before they happen can all make sailing more enjoyable and safer.

Bill Burr's new *Sailing Tips* solves 1,000 problems that can plague any sailboat. This book is a quick study and gives one accurate piece of advice after another ranging from the installation of a CD player to actual testing of a depth sounder compared with the lead line or taking care of your propeller. Some of this information has been buried in cumbersome texts but now is available in a fun, easy to read volume that is useful to anyone who owns a yacht or plans to spend time on the water.

Gary Jobson
Annapolis
January 1989

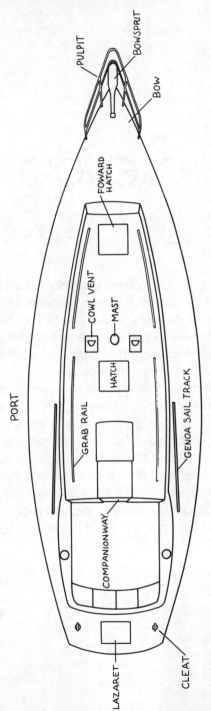

PULPIT

BOWSPRIT

BOW

FOWARD HATCH

COWL VENT

MAST

PORT

GRAB RAIL

HATCH

GENOA SAIL TRACK

STARBOARD

COMPANIONWAY

LAZARET

CLEAT

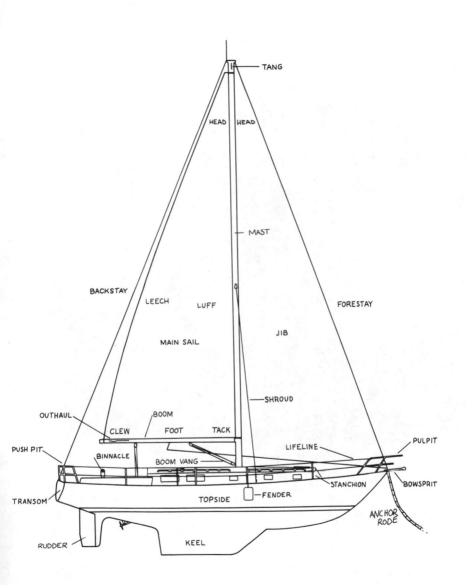

ACKNOWLEDGMENT

I would like to thank the hundreds of sailors whose books and articles I have collected and valued over the years, as well as those who have informally shared their sailing experience. Many of their ideas have been included in these pages. Without their contribution, this book would not have been possible.

I also thank all the many friends whose enthusiasm and knowledge nourished my love of sailing.

And finally, special thanks to my illustrator, Denice Javas, for her long hours and patience while we searched for ways to illustrate difficult sailing concepts.

INTRODUCTION

A single-handed approach to the dock . . . a leaking through-the-hull fitting . . . tired children on board . . . do these sound familiar? We have all found ways to deal with these problems, but have you wondered how other people have solved them? This book is written with the thought of putting together the hundreds of better ideas sailors have been coming up with over the years.

Sailors often have to use their wits to find solutions to unexpected dilemmas. Although specially designed marine products or specialized equipment may be preferred, these are not always immediately available when needed. In the following chapters, there are hundreds of improvised options to consider.

Many of the techniques described in this book are based on firsthand experience; others are derived from accumulated lore. In going through the available literature and piecing together the ideas of fellow sailors, I have made an effort to compile the most useful and practical of their suggestions. Most are no more than that—just hints, some of which may require further investigation before you apply them.

It is our hope that having these ideas at your fingertips will add to your overall cruising pleasure. After scanning these pages, you may wish to keep this book on the boat for easy reference.

Since there are many alternative approaches to dealing with most sailing situations, we encourage you to share your own solutions with us. With an expanded collection of hints, a new edition will be considered.

Now let's dig into the mysteries of electric motors, balky diesels, sail maintenance, singlehanded cruising, and onboard creature comforts. By examining these more than 1,000 ideas gathered from experienced sailors and landlubbers alike, you will find dozens of new hints for better and safer sailing.

CHAPTER 1

~~~~~

ABOVE DECK

The above-deck area certainly gets more use than any other part of the boat. Making this, the hub of activity, safer and more fun is the intention of Part 1, which is divided into four chapters: Life in the Cockpit, Sails to Move By, Better Decks, and Rigging, the Unsung Hero.

LIFE IN THE COCKPIT

Much of the activity on the boat is centered in this intensely small area. Since early days, the cockpit has been the nerve center of all sailing craft. Most decisions, boat control, and community living take place here. Any improvements made to upgrade the crowded, busy cockpit should be universally welcome.

BLOWING CHARTS Keep blowing charts under control in the cockpit by mounting a sandwich of clear acrylic sheets on a hinge (see Figure 1). Slip the chart between the acrylic sheets. Course information can now be marked with a grease pencil on the plastic surface without defacing the chart.

Or try a clipboard as a chart holder. For quick reference, attach it to nearby standing rigging with a snap and lanyard.

FIGURE 1

Alternatively, fold the chart in half and put it in a large 11-by-18-inch Ziploc plastic bag attached to the side of the cockpit bulkhead with Velcro.

PLASTIC CHART COVERS   Seal frequently used charts in clear contact paper. Marks made with a grease pencil on the plastic surface are easily removed.

WEATHERPROOF NOTEPAD   Get a writing clipboard with a Formica top for taking rough notes on course, speed, and weather for later entry in the ship's log and chart when you are below.

SLATE NOTE PAD   Divers use a writing slate and ordinary lead pencil to take notes under water. Since slate is waterproof, easy to mark, and erasable, try using it in the cockpit for temporary course and weather notes.

MASTHEAD INSPECTION   When you use the binoculars, make it a habit to scan the masthead as good maintenance practice. Look for any signs of trouble on the vangs, spreaders, electronic connections, and upper rigging.

ALARM THE CREW   Mount a waterproof button in the cockpit that will sound a buzzer below to summon the crew when you can't leave the helm.

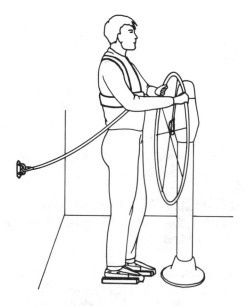

FIGURE 2

SAFE HELMSMAN   Have you thought to put a padeye near the helmsman to secure his safety harness in poor weather and at night?

When the boat heels severely, the helmsman's footing at the wheel is generally not good. Place two very low-profile wood cleats in the cockpit sole at his feet to keep him from sliding to leeward (see Figure 2).

MASTER LIGHT SWITCH   When running at night with lights on in the cockpit, it can help to have a master light switch near the helmsman so that he or she can turn off the cockpit lights for a moment, take a look around, and then turn them on again.

Another idea is to install an automotive rheostat into the circuit. The illumination can then be turned up or down to the desired intensity.

NIGHT VISION   Use the night vision part of your eyes by looking around an object, not directly at it. This will avoid the center blind spot of your eye.

Because it takes up to 30 minutes to develop good night vision, you should do everything possible to preserve it. Keep all cockpit lights, instrument lights, and lights from below to a minimum.

Red lights below do not interfere with night vision or with a sleeping crew. They also help the crew below to adjust their eyes more rapidly when they come on deck.

RED FLASHLIGHT   Keep a red-lensed flashlight handy in the cockpit and the engine room.

NIGHT CHART PROBLEMS   Remember that red markings on the chart do not show up well in red light; green, black, and blue tend to appear best.

KEEP WARM   Use an old skier's trick to warm your hands. Rapidly swing your arms in large circles, like a windmill. This causes the blood to rush to the hands and gives them almost instant warmth.

FROZEN PADLOCK   Tying a plastic sandwich bag around the companionway padlock will help keep it from freezing in the cold of winter.

KEEP COOL   On hot nights, anchor by the stern, putting the open cockpit in the path of the wind.

When at anchor, use the jib halyard to raise an air scoop over the front hatch, bringing cool night air below.

On a very hot day, occasionally throw some water on the deck to keep it cool.

It will help to sail under the genoa alone so that the bimini can remain up to give shade.

DINGHY AS WINDSCOOP   The dinghy can be an effective windscoop. When at anchor, slightly raise the dinghy bow over the forward hatch to funnel fresh air below. Underway, in settled weather, a well-secured overturned dinghy can be a fresh air cover for an open hatch. Promptly return the dinghy to its permanent position if the wind increases.

VENTILATION HATCHES Consider adding deck ventilation hatches to provide more fresh air and light below in the galley and head. Also, add an opening port to the cockpit seat riser to provide ventilation for the coffin-like quarter berth directly below.

DODGER A cockpit dodger can greatly improve sailing comfort. It allows you to stay dry on a cold rainy day or when heavy spray is coming on board. On very hot days, the dodger allows you to keep the companionway hatch open during rain showers.

CONESTOGA AWNING An inexpensive awning can be constructed over the cockpit using bent PVC pipe in Conestoga wagon style. Make a rectangular awning with sleeves sewn into two of the sides. Next place two ½-inch thick PVC pipes into four PVC T-joints run through the lifelines on the port and starboard sides. Before inserting the pipe into the T-joints, slip the awning sleeves over the pipes. This awning and its flexible frame will provide efficient shade.

HOMEMADE GANGPLANK To make coming and going easier when docked "stern to," a gangplank is extremely helpful. Automatically adjusting its height and angle to the dock as the tide changes, it is completely self-tending. It is also easy to raise at night for increased privacy.

A 10-foot aluminum ladder secured and well padded

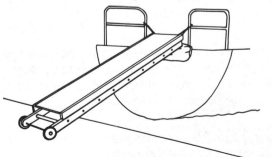

FIGURE 3

can be tied to the stern of the boat. At the dock end of the ladder, drill two holes in the ladder sides and insert an axle and two wheels so the ladder can move freely back and forth on the dock. Secure a piece of plywood that is cut perfectly on top of the ladder rungs to the ladder. This will be the walking surface. With very little effort you have made a strong, efficient and lightweight gangplank (see Figure 3).

INSTANT FIRE STARTER   Barbecue cooking at the stern of the boat provides an enormous expansion of the shipboard menu. However, starting a fire requires extreme caution. *Be sure to keep a fire extinguisher accessible when using the barbecue.* Also be certain that it is not too windy to safely light the fire.

Fatwood is a freak of nature. It has a dense concentration of natural pitch that accumulates only in stumps of virgin longleaf pine. Two sticks start a roaring fire in the barbecue. It is available from most specialty catalog suppliers.

Another quick way to start charcoal is to use a large juice can with both ends cut out. Punch many holes around one end. Place the can upright in the grill, fill the bottom with crushed newspaper, and top with charcoal. Light through the holes. When the charcoal looks well lit, remove the can with pliers or tongs. Place it safely in a bucket of water to cool down and store for reuse.

Or put enough charcoal for one fire in a closed paper bag or empty egg carton. Pop the whole thing onto the grill and light.

Use the inflatable dinghy foot pump to fan the freshly started briquettes. Aim the hose at the fire and after a few strong puffs the coals will glow.

CHARCOAL SAFETY   A recent consumer's magazine advised that wet charcoal can catch fire from spontaneous combustion. It may be wise, therefore, to double-bag your charcoal in waterproof plastic for safety.

LONG MATCHES   Long uncooked pieces of spaghetti do a great job as tapers to light the barbecue.

PROPANE BARBECUE Stainless steel propane grills run by small disposable bottles are getting popular. They reach cooking temperature quickly and have no messy coal residue.

Use approved propane safety procedures, and store the propane bottles in a deck locker.

CLEAN GRILL Clean the barbecue grill by putting it in a plastic garbage bag with plenty of detergent and water. Tie tightly and allow it to soak for a while. Rinse and dry, and you will have a spotless grill.

STEAM CLEAN GRILL Steam the grill clean by wrapping it while still hot in wet newspapers. Use fire retardant gloves to pick up the grill.

CONTROL BLOWING SOOT Keep barbecue soot from blowing all over the boat by dampening the ashes with water from a detergent spray bottle. When you are positive that they are out, scrape the damp ashes into a paper bag for disposal.

FLAVORED BARBECUE Sprinkle water-soaked herbs, apple peels, or onion skins on glowing charcoals for a new flavor.

GOURMET BARBECUE A handy accessory for the gourmet grill is a steel wire fish basket that holds a fish tightly for grilling.

Try unusual BBQ sauces such as Cajun spice blends or mesquite-flavored sauce for a tantalizing new taste. Baste with thin sauces that will not char the way thick sauces do.

Flavor grilled food with wood chips such as alder, hickory, grapevine, sassafras, mesquite, and—the ultimate—chips from whiskey-aged hardwood barrels.

Keep the fire low and hot. Put a pan of beer or wine on the coals; the vapor from it will add flavor and keep the meat moist.

KNUCKLE PROTECTOR Stop burning your hands when you roast marshmallows or hot dogs. Put the stick through an aluminum pie plate, which will shield your hand from the heat.

CRASH PROTECTION   Run a shock cord from underneath a locker lid and clip to a lifeline above to prevent the lid from crashing down on your fingers.

WINCH HANDLE HOLDER   Purchase a short length of soft, clear 2½-inch plastic tubing. Taper one end and attach to the bulkhead. This makes a perfect winch handle holder at almost no cost. The open bottom allows water to drain easily (see Figure 4).

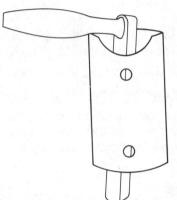

FIGURE 4

SPRAY CURTAINS   Protect the crew from drenching spray by installing canvas curtains on the cockpit lifelines. Pockets can be sewn on the curtains to hold lines, safety harnesses, and oars.

SOFT TOP STEP   Make the top step of the companionway more comfortable for sitting out of the wind by sewing a fitted removable cushion to fit the step.

SCUPPER STRAINERS   Sink drain strainers made of stainless steel, correctly sized, can be excellent debris collectors when they are placed in the cockpit scuppers. They are cheap, easily removed for cleaning, and available at hardware or plumbing supply stores.

LINE STORAGE   Hang all your extra coils of line neatly from leather or Velcro straps in a convenient cockpit lazaret. A few canvas bags can also be hung to hold short pieces of line, cockpit tools, and items for sail repair.

HAND BEARING COMPASS Rubber covered "hockey puck" hand bearing compasses hang comfortably around the neck and are very easy to read. They are quite accurate when used away from metallic interference.

WHEEL WRAPPING Whip some fine cotton twine around the wheel to prevent the cold slippery feel of stainless steel. Straight whipping or half hitches look good and wear well. Use a marking stitch like a turk's head to show by feel when the rudder is exactly at center position.

VINYL WHEEL WRAP A warm, secure, comfortable grip on a stainless wheel is assured if you wrap the wheel with waterproof vinyl chafing tape.

CLOTHESPINS Among the many uses for clothespins are to attach fishing lines to the stays, to clip a chart book open to the correct page, and to hold napkins together in a breezy cockpit.

LIFESLING Be sure to mount the man-overboard pole or Lifesling high enough so a quartering wave will not accidentally launch it.

QUALITY CUSHIONS The best cushions are made of closed-cell foam that is covered with a washable fabric. Because they don't absorb water, they dry quickly after serving as swim floats.

CLEAN CUSHIONS Clean the grime from cockpit cushions by using lemon oil on a rag.

LIFELINE CUSHIONS As crew, we have all spent long hours leaning against the lifelines to put weight on the high side. Relieve this discomfort to the nape of your neck and midback by padding the lifeline with foam tubing. Six-foot sections of split closed-cell tubing are available from plumbing supply stores. Slip these sections over cockpit lifelines to make a comfortable spot to lean against. Hold them fast with duct tape.

HOMEMADE LEAD LINE
Make your own sounding lead by carefully pouring melted lead into a cardboard tube. Put a whiskey bottle cap in the end to mold the arming cavity in the bottom.

LEAD LINE
The seldom used lead line can be employed very effectively on the sailboat.

Determine the water depth ahead of the boat by using the lead line from the dinghy.

Use it to check the accuracy of the depth sounder.

Hang it over the side, just touching the bottom, so that the line will drift at an angle if you are dragging anchor.

Make it function as a low-water alarm. At the deck, attach a bell to the line. Then hang the weight a foot below the deepest part of the keel. The bell will ring when the weight touches bottom.

The wax in the hollow of the weight can show the composition of the bottom before you anchor.

Use the lead line to check depths at an anchorage or dock.

BETTER DECKS

Safety, aesthetics, and sound footing are top priorities for improving boat decks. There are always, however, questions to be asked. Should you change a production boat's winch layout to better suit your crew? Could an additional ventilation hatch make life below on hot days more liveable? Can the foredeck be a safer place for making sail changes in wet weather? The following sections expand on these topics and add tips to increase both pleasure and efficiency.

SPRAY RAILS   Attach spray rails to the cabin top to divert water coming over the cabin off the sides. This will keep the cockpit drier in rough weather.

NAUTICAL RAIN BARREL   To collect fresh water, funnel rain off the cabin top to a bucket lashed on deck. Use wood molding or rolled wet towels to make a V-shaped trough near the rail on the cabin top. Direct the rainwater from the lowest point of the molding or towels through a small plastic hose into a bucket (see Figure 5).

If you prefer, you can rig the sail cover below the main boom to act as a gutter. The rain will run down the raised main into the sail cover and flow to the lowest point and into a bucket.

Another approach is to turn the cockpit awning or bimini into a rain collector. Put a through-the-hull fitting in the center of the bimini at its lowest point. When it rains, connect a garden hose to the bottom of the through-the-hull fitting and deposit the collected water into a container.

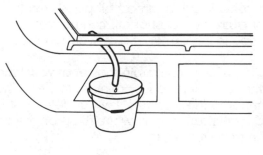

FIGURE 5

PURIFY RAIN WATER   Very carefully used, chlorine bleach or tincture of iodine can purify fresh water. Mix in 10 to 12 drops of 1 percent available chlorine or 5 to 6 drops of 2 percent available tincture of iodine per quart of water and let stand for a minimum of 45 minutes.

DECK SHOWER   A new, unused multigallon insecticide spray tank makes a perfect shower on deck.

JERRY CANS Many uses have been found for the versatile plastic jerry can . . . mostly for holding fuel and water.

To control the jerry can pouring rate, put a finger into the spout and release it when the spout is aimed exactly where needed.

The cans should be clearly marked with the contents and boat name so that they can be found on a cluttered dock.

Wet the deck with water before you pour fuel. That way, if there is a spill, it will be easier to clean topsides and teak.

Adding chlorine bleach to filled water cans stored on deck will help to inhibit marine growth.

PREVENT OVERFLOWING TANKS Prevent overflowing water or fuel tanks by inserting a small device that whistles while you are filling the tank. When the tank is full, air ceases to escape and the whistle stops.

RUBBER BUCKET Why even consider having a galvanized bucket on the boat when molded rubber buckets are available? These can withstand almost all punishment, can't rust, chip, dent or crush and, best of all, can be stored in a semi-collapsed shape in the corner of a crowded lazaret.

LAUNDRY ON DECK Use a rain shower as your laundromat at sea. Let the rain fall for a few minutes to clean the salt off the deck, then stop the scuppers, lay out detergent-sprinkled laundry, and let the rain do the work. Rinse on the other side of the boat in clean rain water.

DRYING CLOTHES A large amount of clothes can be dried in a small space by hanging two parallel lines from bow to stern and using clothespins to clip on clothes crosswise.

Or twist two clotheslines around each other and secure arms and legs of wet clothes in the twists for drying.

Small items such as gloves, socks, and towels will dry more quickly if suspended in a wire basket in the warm engine room.

LAZY CREW Wide comfortable hammocks made with soft, strong, flexible cotton rope have a universal appeal for loafing in luxury on deck. Sling the hammock between the mast and any convenient shroud for hours of perfect relaxation. When they are not in use, hammocks store in almost no space at all.

BEVERAGE HOLDER It is easy to make a beverage holder that can be attached to a lifeline or any other convenient spot. Shape single-strand electrical wire around a beer can or glass. Form a hook at the top of the beverage holder. Because the wire is so stiff, it can be shaped to fit almost any small object you wish to hang (see Figure 6).

TEAK FACTS Teak is an extraordinary wood. Because it absorbs little water, it does not swell, split, or warp easily. It's easy to shape and takes a wonderful finish. Resistance to most marine fungi and insects is high.

Most of us either varnish, treat, or leave teak alone. Three coats of varnish as a base with occasional sanding and revarnishing will keep the finish going for months. If you prefer unvarnished teak, there are hundreds of commercial cleaners, bleaches, brighteners, and oils on the market. The least energetic person will probably choose to leave the teak alone, giving it only an occasional detergent scrubbing. Below in the cabin, unvarnished clean teak responds well to lemon oil furniture polish.

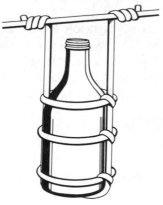

FIGURE 6

CLEANING TEAK   Mix powdered commercial teak cleaner with enough water to form a paste. This will prevent the cleaner from blowing away.

In the absence of a commercial cleaner, make a paste of bleach and household cleansing powder. Apply this paste to the teak, let dry, and rinse off.

Try using dry talcum powder to soak up grease spots from raw teak.

LAST RESORT   TSP (trisodium phosphate) can be used as a last resort to clean up an unsightly wood deck. It is very strong and should be used carefully and in moderation, following the manufacturer's directions. Brush TSP into a small area of soiled wood, and rinse thoroughly when the original color of the wood shows again.

SPOT CLEANING TEAK   Occasionally there is a localized stain on oiled teak. Spray the spot with a household cleaner, blot with a paper towel, lightly sand and re-oil.

NONSKID DECK   Wet or dry, one of the best nonskid deck surfaces is untreated teak.

NONSKID TAPE   Rolls of nonskid tape can be applied to improve safety on bowsprits, ladder treads, spreader tops, cockpit coamings, swim ladders, and boarding areas.

DECK LEAK   When you look for a deck leak, remember that water flows to the lowest point. Therefore, the problem begins above the spot where you see the leak. Hose down individual deck fittings, starting at the lowest, until the leak shows in the cabin. Make your repair outside, not below.

BEDDING COMPOUND   Before applying bedding compound, mask the areas not to be covered. Spread the compound on both surfaces of the materials to be set together. Screw it down in stages so that the compound is not squeezed out.

Scribe a groove into uncured bedding compound to encourage water runoff.

WOOD PLUG REMOVAL
Wood plugs can often be removed using an ice pick.

Plugs will be easier to remove if they are set with varnish rather than glue.

CLEAN METALWORK
Deck metalwork cannot stay in perfect shape without regular care. Hose it down frequently with fresh water, wipe it dry, and apply metal polish.

SPINNAKER POLE USES
The spinnaker pole can be used to lift the dinghy on board or bring heavy supplies into the cockpit. Put extra padeyes on both sides of the mast to support the spinnaker pole.

Wing out the staysail with the spinnaker pole on one side and the genoa on the other side for wing and wing downwind sailing.

Winging out two headsails with aluminum poles often leads to a broken pole. Try using a 16-foot carbon fiber sailboard mast for this job. Conventional pole ends fit in the carbon fiber mast.

FIGURE 7

CLIMBING ALOFT An emergency way to go aloft is to shinny up a pair of parallel shrouds by wrapping a leg around each shroud. Be sure to wear long pants and gloves as you climb (see Figure 7).

Another way aloft is to lower the mainsail slightly and carefully use as steps the pockets of sail above the hanks.

A third emergency way aloft is to tie loops every few feet in a strong line and hoist it aloft. When this line is wrapped tightly around the mast as often as possible, the loops make good foot and hand holds to the lower spreaders.

Climbing aloft is always a dangerous job and should be performed with assistance and great care.

LOOKOUT ALOFT Install nonskid strips on the upper side of the spreader to give a lookout safer footing.

SPREADER LIGHTS Add lights to the upper side of the spreader. With these lights turned on, the top of the mast and upper rigging can be inspected at night.

DECK LAMPS Save unnecessary power drain on the boat's batteries by carefully and more frequently using self-contained lighting.

Coleman-style lanterns can provide a great deal of light, in fact up to 125 candlepower for three hours. Try using one for repair work at night, picnics ashore, or cooking at the barbecue.

Butane lamps can also provide good light away from the electrical system and are not as short-lived as battery-operated lamps.

Cyalume sticks give off a green glow for up to eight hours after they are bent, snapped, and shaken. They are waterproof, require no power source, and are small enough to pack anywhere.

MORSE CODE LIGHTS Now available is a small switching unit that can be easily wired into the circuit of the 360-degree white navigation light. When activated, it causes the light to flash the Morse code "V," which stands for "I require assistance."

DIRTY SHOES   Cure the ever-present problem of returning to the boat with dirt and pebbles stuck in shoe soles by getting a shoe scraper made of super-tough nylon bristles. Bolt it down to the dock where the boat is boarded. A quick scrape across the bristles will remove the troublesome dirt.

DRAIN CLEANER   A kitchen basting syringe can be used to clean out dirty scuppers, deck drains, and clogged anchor wells. Separate the rubber bulb from the syringe and use the bulb as a miniature plumbers' helper at the sink and cockpit drains.

TOPSIDE CLEANING   A clever way to clean the topsides is to get in the dinghy and hold onto the sailboat with your hand. By putting a long-handled brush in the oarlock, you can use a back and forth motion to brush the topsides clean (see Figure 8).

Detergent and salt water brushed on the boottop will remove the oil that stains the water line.

FIGURE 8

PILING HOOK   Rusty nails on the piling are a menace to your boat and you. Buy some heavy-duty, single-strand, plastic-covered electric wire. Make a Z-shaped hook from the wire and attach it to the piling. This is a lot safer and does an excellent job of holding the docking lines.

BETTER PULPIT DESIGN   Improve the safety of the foredeck by repositioning the pulpit just short of the jibstay. This will provide better footing and cause less chafing on the jib.

Mounting the running lights on the pulpit will prevent them from being blanketed by the jib.

Run the lifelines to the pulpit rather than to the foredeck as an improved safety feature.

NONSKID BOWSPRIT   Put nonskid plastic strips or nonskid paint on the top of the bowsprit, which is often wet and slippery.

Install a sailboard toe strap on the bowsprit for better footing forward.

FIGHTING CHAFE   Preventing chafe is a constant battle that can be won by taping all cotter pins, spreader ends, and lifelines.

Try using clear, flexible plastic tubing as chafe protection for dock lines and anchor ropes.

ELECTROLYSIS   Corrosion from electrolysis occurs when two dissimilar metals are in contact with each other in a salt environment. Using rubber gaskets, plastic sheets, or bedding compound to separate unlike metals creates a barrier and gives protection from electrolysis.

GOOD LUBRICANTS   Grease for water pumps does an excellent job of lubricating rudder pintles, hatch hinges, anchor shackles, and turnbuckles.

Anhydrous lanolin is a nonwater-soluble lubricant that works very well. Use it on screw heads, shackle threads, turnbuckles, snapshackles, slide bolt latches, adjustable wrenches, and any place where rust prevention is required.

RECOVERING DROPPED EQUIPMENT   As soon as an item is inadvertently dropped over the side of an anchored boat, drop a weight on a string to the bottom. When a swimmer goes down, the weighted string will show exactly where the lost item is located.

Small magnets with 50-pound holding power can be dropped over the side on a lanyard to fish for lost key rings, tools, or other ferrous metal objects.

WINCH HANDLES   Improve winch leverage by purchasing new handles that are at least 10 inches long. Double-grip handles let you put both hands on for a better hold.

ALTERNATIVE WINCH   Try an old whaler's trick called *swigging* to tighten a line. If there is no mast winch, take a turn around the cleat with the halyard, then reach up and pull the halyard out as far as possible. With the other hand, pull the halyard taut at the cleat for a gain of a few inches each time the procedure is repeated.

WINCH HANDLING   Always remember that winches are power-increasing tools and create tremendous pressures on the line. Approach every winch-handling job with your full attention and concern for safety.

Load the winch with two or three clockwise wraps. Watch the sail, not the winch, and stop tightening when the sail no longer luffs.

Release small amounts of sheet by cupping one hand around the wraps and feeding the line out with the other. To release the sheet completely, pull it straight up off the drum.

If more power is needed, double winch by putting a couple of turns around one winch and feeding the line to a second winch on the other side. A person will be required on each winch.

WINCH CARE   Frequent fresh water rinsings will flush out accumulated salt from winches. When disassembly is required for winch maintenance, be careful when removing the drum because bearings can stick to the inside and drop overboard. Most internal parts can be washed with kerosene.

LUBRICATING WINCHES A good sign that a winch needs care is when you hear muted clicks rather than loud metal clicks when the winch is turned.

Follow the manufacturer's instructions when lubricating winches. Be cautious not to use detergent oils because they will probably corrode any brass or bronze in the winch.

HATCH GASKETS It is very difficult to obtain replacement gaskets for hatches and ports. Regular household window gasket material, available at hardware stores, may solve the problem.

MAST STEP CARE The mast step is particularly subject to corrosion from the water that often collects in the area. After removing the corrosion, paint with a zinc chromate primer for future protection.

HOMEMADE MAST BOOT After cutting a truck inner tube in half like a bagel, cut one of the pieces in half like the letter C. Wrap it around the mast step, overlapping the ends, and bind it top and bottom with steel strapping. Cover with a tie-on dress boot of the same material as is used for sail covers.

MAST RAILING Safety at the mast is improved if you install railings as handholds on each side of the mainmast.

MAST WINCHES Find a spot on the mast to mount the winches high enough to allow you to stand and crank, yet low enough so that the winches can be reached while you sit with your legs straddling the mast for support. This option will be welcome on a rough day when you are working alone at the mast.

BIRD CHASER At the mooring, do birds regularly roost on your rigging and make a mess of the deck? Recently advertised is a thin stiff tape which, when stretched taut between two points, vibrates in the slightest breeze. The resulting ultrasonic hum makes the birds go elsewhere to rest. Thin strapping tape may work just as well.

OCEAN RACING INNOVATIONS   The big singlehanded ocean races have contributed a number of innovations for the cruising sailor.

Small windvanes are being linked to the autopilot to control headings by apparent wind rather than by compass.

Sail stoppers take line tension off winches. Therefore, using a few sail stoppers can reduce the number of winches on deck.

Trim tabs can be used on the rudder to help the autopilot move easily, using much less power.

Color-coded lines are being seen more frequently to solve common line mixups.

SAILS TO MOVE BY

Sailors love their boats because of the majesty of sail compared with the noise and odor of engine power. Not all sailors understand the physical dynamics of movement by sail, but they do appreciate the tremendous forces at work to propel the boat through the sea. In the next section there are a few dozen new and improved ideas on the handling, care, and repair of sails.

GENERAL CARE   Dacron is the most prevalent sailcloth used today and requires fairly simple maintenance. A silicone coating on the cloth acts as a soil barrier and helps resist wear from chafing. Salt is highly abrasive and holds moisture, allowing mildew to form on dirt embedded in sails. You can remove surface dirt by washing the sails with household detergent and water. Because most detergents are alkaline, which is damaging to Dacron, thoroughly rinse the sails after washing.

Hang the wet sails on a line if possible. Drying on the boat is not a good idea because of probable flogging and chafing.

SPECIFIC CARE   Most common stains can be removed from sails. Use great care and always test before proceeding.

Rust. Try to keep the soiled area wet. First try to clean with lemon juice. Then, if that is not successful, use detergent and, as a last resort, a weak solution of oxalic acid. Use oxalic acid very carefully, following proper label precautions. Rinse thoroughly.

Blood stains. Again, try to keep the spot wet. Run cold sea or fresh water over the stain for up to half an hour until it is gone. If it still shows, work in some detergent paste made with cold water, and rinse thoroughly.

Mud and grass stains. Mild detergent and thorough rinsing will remove these stains most of the time.

Mildew. First try lemon juice. If that does not work, very carefully use detergent and bleach. Rinse very well; bleach is destructive of Dacron.

Creosote and oil. Not much can be done with creosote or oil stains other than scraping off the excess and, after testing carefully, using rubbing alcohol, trichlorethylene, or mineral spirits on the spot. Very careful bleaching and rinsing may remove any remaining stain.

SALTY CANVAS
Just a few minutes of a tropical downpour will flush the salt out of the sails or their covers. The spinnaker will be noticeably lighter and more efficient. The main will be clean and ready to use as a scoop for catching rainwater.

HOISTING SAIL ON DECK
A large bagged headsail can be very difficult to drag onto the foredeck from below. Hook a halyard to the sailbag, and winch it up through the forehatch.

CLIPPED BAG
Tie the sailbag to a foredeck stanchion using a lanyard attached to the bottom of the bag. The sail will be easier to remove, and the empty bag will not blow away.

BAGGING THE HEADSAIL
It is not difficult to have a sailbag made with zippered sides. Tie it unzipped to a foredeck stanchion to receive a lowered sail. Zip it up, and you have a bagged sail ready to go at a moment's notice.

If a headsail is to be bagged and stored below, first flake the sail neatly along the side deck. Then, starting at the clew end, fold it forward in an accordion or roadmap fashion. Folded in this manner, the sail will slide easily into its bag.

STOW SAILS ON DECK
An excellent way to keep a lowered headsail from ballooning up on deck is to fold it along the rail and tie it to the lifeline stanchions with three or four sailstops.

GENOA TRACK MARKS
Mark with paint the number of every fifth genoa track hole so that the preferred position for each of your headsails can be recorded and instantly selected.

As an alternative idea, place tape on the deck by each headsail car position. Mark the tape with the name of the sail to be used at that position.

GENOA REEF
The genoa track snatch block must be relocated when you reef the genoa. Move the genoa car until the sheet and the genoa miter form an imaginary straight line.

REDUCING HEADSAIL
Reefing a roller furling genoa in heavy weather does not solve the problem of too much headsail. The remaining sail will be too high and far forward for good balance. Consider a removable stay that is attached about two-thirds of the way up the mast and run down to the foredeck. A small staysail hanked to this stay will give the boat much better balance. A boomless staysail works well and reduces gear on the foredeck.

If there is no alternative to reefing a roller furling headsail, move the sheet leads as far forward as possible.

REEFING THE MAIN
Lower the mainsail to each reefing position in no-wind conditions, and mark the halyard and reefing lines for easy reference. In heavy weather, it will help to run a line up to the mainsail reefing grommet and back down to a winch. Even though there is a load on the main, it can be winched down to the reefing position.

Using a staysail with a reefed main reduces the sail area to a manageable size.

LACING THE LIFELINE
Lace the forward lifelines in a triangular fashion with heavy line to keep lowered sails on board and to improve foredeck safety.

SAIL HANDLING
Install a third lifeline on the foredeck to keep headsails from going over the side.

Put handrails over dorado deck cowl vents to keep sheets from catching.

RAISING THE HEADSAIL IN STOPS
A safe way to raise a headsail in heavy weather is to have previously cinched the sail at each hank with a rubberband. Take the sail forward, clip it on the forestay, and attach the sheets and halyard. Raise the sail and, from the cockpit, sheet it in. This will break the rubberband sailstops and set the sail without flogging any crewmembers.

SETTING THE SPINNAKER
Shorthanded crews can get great benefit from a cruising spinnaker.

When you remove the spinnaker from its bag, it is easier to orient it if it has been marked with colored tape—red tape on starboard luff, green on port luff, and white on the foot. Tie spinnaker sheets to the clews rather than using metal shackles. A good knot is less likely to open accidentally.

A spinnaker can be set without having a large crew on the foredeck by using the following procedure. Run the sheets and guy to the cockpit, but feed the other running rigging to the mast winches. Before setting the spinnaker, cleat the guy, topping lift, and downhaul. Sail below a beam reach with a tightly trimmed genoa. Now, set the spinnaker from the lee side in the shadow of the main.

To drop the spinnaker, use the genoa to backwind it on a beam reach. Move the pole forward to the head stay before releasing the guy shackle. Release the halyard slowly, and collect the spinnaker on the lee deck.

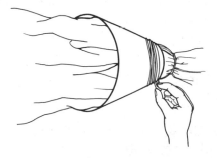

FIGURE 9

SIMPLIFIED SPINNAKER LAUNCHING
Cinching the spinnaker with rubberbands for easier launching is a big job. An easy way to get these rubber bands on the sail is to slip 15 to 20 large rubber bands onto the small end of a big plastic funnel. The small end of the funnel should be cut off leaving a large enough hole for the sail to be easily pulled through. As the chute is fed through the small end of the funnel, the rubber bands are slipped from the funnel to the spinnaker at the desired intervals (see Figure 9).

There are poleless cruising spinnakers that come with a furling sock. The sock containing the spinnaker is raised with the halyard and peels up over the sail head as the chute fills.

SPINNAKER HANDLING
While the spinnaker is up, tie off the bitter end of the spinnaker halyard. The coiled halyard will be much less likely to kink than if it were free.

If the spinnaker ends up in the water, be sure that one corner is released so that the sail will not hold water and put a strain on the gear.

SPINNAKER TRIM
Put telltales along the spinnaker leaches to aid in trimming.

FORESAIL CHAFE
Sew a sacrificial patch on the sail and also on the pulpit where chafing occurs. The patches can be

replaced as they wear through. Use sailmaker's liquid plastic, brushing it over the stitches to increase their resistance to chafe and ultraviolet (UV) deterioration.

Getting high-cut jibs reduces the chafe on the foot of the foresail.

SLIPPERY DACRON   Try not to walk on slippery Dacron sails lying on deck.

MAINSAIL TRIMMING   Use magnetic tape or colored yarn as telltales. Attach them to the sail with sail repair tape. Put the port and starboard telltales at slightly different heights for the best observation. The windward telltale will flutter when you are trimmed too tight. The leeward ones will fly about when you are sailing too loose. If you have battens, the first or second batten should be parallel to the boom when the mainsail is correctly trimmed.

Too much weather helm slows the boat. Having a deep main, the traveler to weather and a tight trim will accentuate weather helm. Under most conditions, more than 4 degrees of weather helm is very detrimental to speed. Mark your wheel at 2, 4, and 6 degrees to be aware of this phenomenon when it occurs.

DEPOWERING THE MAIN   The fastest and easiest way to depower the main in a puff is to drop the ball bearing traveler down to leeward momentarily. Ball bearing travelers can be adjusted quite easily when under load. It is more difficult if you choose to ease the sheet temporarily and then have to fight it back in again.

FULLY BATTENED MAIN   Racing rules have discouraged the use of fully battened mains. They are, however, very effective. The battens are not difficult for a sailmaker to install on your present main. The modified sail will give better sail performance as a result of its improved shape. Also, the sails should last longer because they will no longer flog easily.

SAILSTOP THE MAIN   Neatly stow the main by having one crew member slowly lower the sail while two others in the crew fold it in flakes across the boom. When it is partly down, put a sail stop at the clew. When it is two-thirds down, put a stop at the luff. Finally, stop the head at the middle of the boom.

DAMAGE INSPECTION   Inspect the sails regularly by spreading them on the ground and checking all the seams, pockets, patches, ropes, fasteners, and hardware. Mark with colored tape any chafe spots, tears, stains, or broken stitching.

If you do find problems and the sails need to be reshaped by the sailmaker, make his job easier by photographing them from the deck up to show camber and from the stern when they are close-hauled to show the sheeting angle.

As an added precaution against a blown seam, after a few years of sail wear, add a third row of stitches between the sailmaker's double row of stitches.

EMERGENCY PATCHES   Self-sticking sail repair patches placed on both sides of the sail do a good job for temporary repairs. Stitching the patch at a later time makes the repair even better.

Another method of temporary repair is to wash, rinse, and dry the sail area to be fixed. Apply contact cement to both the patch and the sail. Place them together; when they are partly dry, press or hammer the edges firmly. In an hour or so the sail will be ready to go. You can make quick temporary repairs on Mylar and Kevlar with sticky-backed insignia cloth used by sailmakers to make sail numbers.

BARBERHAULING   Barberhauling is a method of adjusting the clew of the jib inboard to improve headsail performance.

A temporary barberhauler can be set up by leading the slack, unused jibsheet around the mast and tightening up on a windward winch. This will have the effect of bringing the jib clew inboard for better trim.

A block and tackle or a second genoa track inboard of the present one provides a good permanent arrangement.

WAX OUTHAUL TRACK   Apply paraffin dissolved in solvent into the nooks and crannies of the mainsail outhaul to ease its movement when under way. Wax the outhaul track and the sail slugs on the bolt rope.

MARK SAIL CORNERS   Use indelible ink to mark each corner of the sail with its name—head, tack, or clew. This is especially helpful when changing sails at night.

RIGGING, THE UNSUNG HERO

When all else is considered, a sound hull and strong rigging are the keys to a safe boat. Rigging, unglamorous yet essential in its importance, requires the watchfulness and attention of a concerned skipper. In the following section, there are many ideas for improving the safety of handling lines and preventing common rigging problems.

BAD WRAP   A bad wrap on a sheet winch always seems to come at the worst possible time. It can be cleared in a few moments if the free sheet is led around the lee side of the mast to a windward winch. Putting a strain on this sheet will slacken the jammed sheet. It should now be fairly easy to undo and reset the leeward winch.

STORING LINE   Get messy halyard tails out from underfoot by storing them in a large sailcloth bag hung over the boom near the mast. Similar bags attached to each corner of the cockpit can store sheet tails. Put the dinghy anchor line in a small bag in the dinghy. Extra docking lines stored in a lazaret in this manner are ready to use without the prospect of fouling.

SECURE HALYARD   If the halyard is expected to remain secured for some time, try running the halyard around the cleat, back up and through the shackle, then down again to be secured on the same cleat.

BELAYING PINS Belaying pins in pinrails, though old-fashioned, are still very effective for cleating lines. First wrap the line around the pin, then make a few S-turns just as you do with cleats.

MODERN PINRAIL Racing boats often bolt three-legged stainless handrails on either side of the mast. These have many uses, including giving the crew something to lean against. Attach a heavy teak crossbar to the legs to create a step and pinrail, an arrangement that gives better access to the top of the sailcover when you are tying it down. It can also provide an excellent vantage point for a crewmember when "eyeballing" through a tricky passage. Additional small lines and halyards can easily be attached to the crossbar as needed.

HALYARD ALOFT Once in a while, as the halyard is being clipped on, it escapes to fly tauntingly out of reach. To recover the halyard, head the boat into the wind. The halyard will blow back over the center of the boat where you can catch it by hand.

Or, tie a large noose on a nearby halyard and lasso the lost halyard.

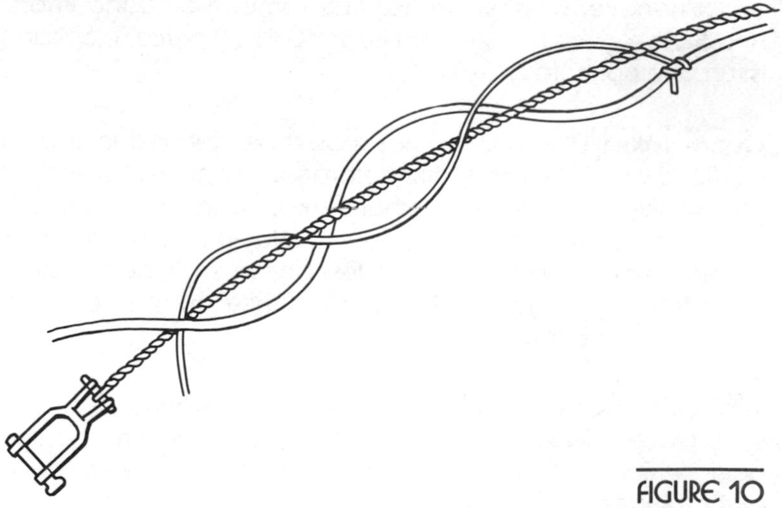

FIGURE 10

Another possibility is to tie a long line to a spare halyard, raise them together, and plait these two around the lost halyard until it is caught and can be lowered (see Figure 10).

HANGING HALYARD COILS   After a halyard is coiled, reach through the middle of the coil and grab the standing part of the line. Pull this as a loop out through the coil, and with a twist, loop it back over the cleat for a perfect hanging coil.

RATLINES   Rope ladders that are mounted along the shrouds from the deck to the spreaders make going aloft easier. Easier access encourages more frequent masthead inspections. Ratlines are especially useful in the tropics for navigation in shoal water.

LINE AND ROPE FACTS   Selecting the proper type of line to use for each application is pretty cut and dried. Remember that about 99 percent of line failure comes from chafe, so protecting line from wear is time well spent.

Most synthetic line becomes stabilized after about 50 cycles of loading and unloading.

Sheaves should be about 10 percent larger than the rope diameter because lines tend to flatten under load.

Whenever possible, splice line rather than using knots. Knots can reduce line strength from 40 to 50 percent. Splicing is fun and not hard to learn.

CLEANING LINES   Dirty lines should be cleaned in a bath tub filled with water and mild detergent. Do not use bleach; it can weaken and discolor synthetic lines. During the rinse, add a small amount of fabric softener, then lay the lines out to dry. The lines will be both clean and less abrasive on the hands.

After cleaning the lines, loosely flake them in a figure eight along a lifeline to dry.

WHIPPING ROPE ENDS   To make the best whipped rope end, place a looped end of waxed cord parallel to the line being whipped. With the loop overlapping the cut end, make eight turns around the loop, then go down through the loop and pull taut. The length of the wraps taken around a line should be equal to the diameter of the line.

There are effective alternative ways to whip synthetic rope ends. The simplest method is to bind the end with adhesive tape for a short-term cure.

Holding the end of a synthetic rope over a flame and shaping it with gloved fingers is another simple technique. Easier on the fingers is to tape some paper on the end, cut the paper flush, and hold over a flame until the end fuses. Plastic shrink tubing pulled over the end and cut flush shrinks tight when held over heat.

TEMPORARY EYE
Tie a small loop in the line, using a marlinspike hitch. Insert a thimble into the loop, and pull it tight to create a temporary eye.

PREVENT LINE TWIST
Coiling line that has been manufactured with a right hand lay will be easier if you coil it clockwise.

The best way to prevent hockles from occurring in new rope is to be sure that it is properly removed from the rope spool. Pull the rope off a free-running spool that is mounted on a rod. Don't buy rope that has slipped off one end of the spool; hockles are certain to develop.

REMOVING LINE TWIST
Tow a badly twisted line behind the boat until it unwinds.

LINE HANDLING
Use a broad tip marker to mark common settings on each sheet.

Don't leave lines for long periods in cam cleats because this wears out the cleat's internal springs.

SAIL TRACK SWITCH
There are times during a big blow when a heavy weather main or storm trysail is necessary but very difficult to rig. Install parallel sail tracks below the entry point for the main. The main can be loaded on one track and the storm trysail on the other. By using a swivel piece of track, you can lower the main onto its track and immediately raise the trysail onto the mast track.

SAIL TRACK OILERS   Keep the sail track running smoothly by using a sail track oiler. This is nothing more than an extra sail slide with an oil-soaked felt attached. Tie this additional slide just below the top slide so that each time the sail is raised or lowered the oiler will lubricate the sail track.

CLEANING WIRE   Tie a cloth soaked in detergent to the shroud. Attach a halyard to the top and a long line to the bottom of the cloth. Pull the cloth up with the halyard and down with the line to clean the shroud.

CUTTING WIRE   Before cutting wire with wire cutters or a cold chisel, whip the wire on either side of the cut to stop any possible unraveling. Be sure to tie down wire under tension so that it does not fly around after it is cut.

WIRE EYE   Nicropress eyes with heavy-duty thimbles should be examined for possible structural deformation when under load. Even the sturdiest of these can deform slightly under the pin area. This deformation will not occur if the space inside the eye is filled. A local metalworker can make a solid bronze thimble to insert in place of a normal thimble.

EMERGENCY WIRE EYE   To make a wire eye, loop the wire around a thimble and secure the standing parts tightly with two wire clamps.

INEXPENSIVE WIRE   It is normally ill-advised to use cheap wire on a boat. However, in an emergency, plastic covered wire will stand up well in noncritical places. Any rusting that starts can be immediately seen through the clear plastic covering.

WHISKER CHECK   Probably the best way to check for broken ends on wire is to wrap a cloth around the wire and rub up and down. Any wire whiskers will snag the cloth.

STRAIGHTEN STANCHION   Bends in stanchions caused by unplanned bumps can be straightened with a plumber's tube bender found at plumbing supply houses.

FAIRLEAD ON STANCHION If you mount a fairlead on a stanchion, small lines such as the foreguy lead or the roller furling line will have clear running space.

PELICAN HOOK FORESTAY There are proprietary release levers such as pelican hooks that do a good job of setting adequate tension on a removable headstay. This is an excellent set up for a temporary staysail headstay.

Chain binders, used on trucks, are helpful to lock down a broken stay that is too short to use.

ADJUSTABLE GENOA CARS A recently developed system allows you to change the genoa car's position under load. In place of the normal genoa track, it employs a traveler track and adjustable cars that are moved by a block-and-tackle arrangement.

SAFER LIFELINES Any of the following ideas should improve the safety of your lifelines:

Replace stanchion tubing with stainless pipes and weld them to the socket with gussets.

Replace the set screws with through bolts.

Replace the lifeline wire with rigging wire.

MAST SHEAVE BOXES When spars are rigged with sheaves, square holes are normally cut in the mast. Cracks can begin at the corners if they were not carefully rounded. Inspect one sheave to see if this is the case. Round the corners if needed. If cracks have begun, have a professional weld performed.

SPAR FASTENINGS Do not use metal screws or self-tapping screws when attaching fittings to a spar. They can leave sharp, potentially damaging edges inside the spar. Rivets or machine screws are very reliable and will not cause damage to internal rigging and wiring.

TUNING RIGGING Generally speaking, a mast should be tuned with a bend in the center under no-load conditions.

Under medium- to high-wind conditions, the mast will straighten, flattening the main and reducing weather helm.

Either a mechanical or hydraulic backstay adjuster can contribute to better performance by adjusting the tension of the rigging. A tight setting creates a taut forestay for neater and easier roller furling. Loosening the adjustment will cause forestay sag, improving genoa performance in light air.

Stays under proper tension should make a dull thudding sound, not a musical note, when struck.

INSPECTING RIGGING   Stress cracks will show on swage fittings if they are rubbed with black shoe polish or Mercurochrome. If you do find a crack, slip a wire through the turnbuckle and clamp it to the stay above as a temporary measure.

By using a jeweler's loupe strapped to your forehead, you can perform magnified rigging inspection with both hands free.

CHEMICAL RIGGING INSPECTION   There is a fairly new chemical compound for checking tangs and mast fittings for hairline cracks and metal fatigue. When it is sprayed on a fitting, any crack or fault will appear. This product is called Ardrox sold by Vresco-Ardrox, 10603 Midway Avenue, Cerritos, CA 90701.

SHARPEN TEETH   Routine inspection will show if camcleat and sheet stopper jaws are rounded off from wear. A triangular file will sharpen these teeth with little effort.

STOP BANGING BLOCK   One of the most annoying sounds on the boat is a slack jib sheet block banging on the deck. Run a shock cord from the block to the lifeline above to hold it off the deck.

BALL BEARING BLOCKS   Use friction reducers to make travelers, blocks, and genoa cars easier to move under load. They don't need lubrication, just an occasional flush with fresh water.

ANHYDROUS LANOLIN   All rigging pins should be well lubricated. Drugstore anhydrous lanolin is waterproof, sticks well to metal, and allows pins to be easily turned by fingers.

LOCTITE   Screws in spreaders and tangs should be made fast by using Loctite.

CLEVIS AND COTTER PINS   Cotter pins should be 1½ times the clevis pin diameter and never spread more than 20 degrees. A small countersink on the cotter pin entry hole will make it easier to insert.

Taping the cotter pin ends saves tearing sails and shins.

Try replacing cotter pins with a stainless steel fisherman's snap that has no jagged edges and closes like a safety pin.

TURNBUCKLES   If all turnbuckles are installed with right-hand threads facing down, there will never be any confusion when tightening or loosening is needed. All open-barreled turnbuckles should have pins in the threaded ends to prevent twisting from opening the turnbuckle.

EASY-OPENING SHACKLE   It is not easy to open the spring-loaded pin of a snap shackle with cold, stiff fingers. Cure this problem by tying a small lanyard to the spring-loaded ring. Even when you are wearing gloves, a pull on the lanyard will open the shackle.

HYDRAULIC POWER   Commercial fishermen have for years been using hydraulics on their boats. Consider using more of this labor-saving technology as it becomes available to cruising sailors. Wherever there is mechanical movement, hydraulics can be applied. Boom vangs, centerboards, backstay tensioners, refrigerators, air conditioners, and winches can all be run by an engine pump to create the hydraulic pressure needed.

TENSION ADJUSTMENT   The slipknot used to tie down the dodger, or bimini, has a tendency to lose its tension. To eliminate this problem, tie a loop on the lanyard about a foot above the deck. Run the end of the lanyard through the deck fitting, up through the loop, and tie with a slipped hitch. With this knot, the tension can be adjusted and untied with a pull.

SOUNDPROOF MAST

Prevent the slapping of internal wiring by inserting a 1¼-inch PVC pipe into the mast. Because of its flexibility, PVC pipe is the perfect container for wiring. Run a few extra wires through the mast for installing new electronic equipment in the future.

Another approach is to bundle the wires and tape them to a length of stiff wire that is a few feet longer than the mast. The longer wire, when inserted, will coil around the inner walls of the mast. This will keep the wires in place and prevent the annoying slapping noise.

REPLACING INTERNAL HALYARDS

In an emergency, you can rig a temporary halyard if you have previously installed an external cheekblock at the masthead.

Short of any other arrangement, a crewmember can drop a fishing sinker on a long monofilament fishing line through the masthead opening. After you remove the opening cover at the bottom of the mast, you can pull the fishing line out with a wire and run a new halyard through.

After the mast is down, tie a messenger line to the end of the halyard. In this way, when you remove the halyard for repair, the messenger line will be pulled through. If you neglected to run a messenger line through, rent an electrician's snake to replace the internal halyards.

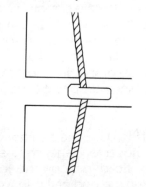

FIGURE 11

SLAPPING HALYARDS   Normally, tying halyards to the shrouds with shock cords prevents slapping noises. Another way to solve this problem is to mount thumb cleats on the spreaders a foot out from the mast. The halyard will slip into the thumb cleats as it is dragged out along the spreader (see Figure 11). It can then be tied down tightly.

Next time the mast is down, slide preformed slotted foam tubing inside the mast. Tape sections together as you insert them. The tubes make good sound insulation to prevent the noise of slapping internal halyards.

JAMMED HALYARD AND ROLLER FURLER   Occasionally the spinnaker halyard gets tangled on the forestay roller furler. To prevent this problem, bring the spinnaker halyard aft outside the shrouds and cleat it tightly to the mast.

TRAPPED SPINNAKER HALYARD   If the halyard gets trapped on the wrong side of the spinnaker pole, tie it to the jib sheet and pass it over the top of the pole to the correct side.

BOOM GUY   One of the problems encountered when using a boom guy to hold a furled main is that in a swell it rocks back and forth causing noise and chafe. Run a tight line from one deck cleat, around the boom, to an opposing deck cleat to prevent this aggravating motion.

TURNBUCKLE COVERS   PVC electrical conduit can be used as chafe protection for turnbuckles, for shroud rollers, and for electrical wiring.

PAINT SPREADER TOPS   Varnish doesn't last long on wooden spreaders. However, if you paint the spreader tops with white paint, this coating will far outlast varnish because of its better resistance to light.

SPREADER CHAFE   Molded rubber or plastic tips on the spreader offer the most permanent protection from chafe. Consider taping the spreader ends heavily to do the same job.

CHAFING TAPE Keep chafing tape from loosening and blowing in the breeze by applying some silicone sealant over the tape ends.

TOPPING LIFT CHAFE Loose topping lifts can saw their way through mainsail stitching by constantly rubbing back and forth. Run a shock cord from the topping lift to a lower shroud to prevent this problem.

CHAPTER 2

~~~~~~

UPKEEP

Now that we have looked at the above-deck area, let's get down to the nitty-gritty and take a hard look at boat upkeep. In this chapter we discuss special tools that can serve double duty, ideas for the layup and commissioning process, and various specific repairs. Finally, we list a variety of effective methods to clean and polish the innumerable materials on board that corrode, rust, or get dirty.

RIGHT TOOL—GOOD JOB

Differing from the cluttered collection of odds and ends found at home, a sailor's toolkit usually contains a selection of carefully chosen items, most of them capable of doing more than one job. Here are a number of ways to use these tools in better and more effective ways.

TOOLBOX Assemble a plastic toolbox of multipurpose tools for the boat. At home you can afford wide variety and duplication, but on the boat you need a few very specific tools. Select noncorrosive tools made from stainless steel, vanadium, or chrome plating to avoid rust. Those of mild steel that you must keep should be coated with WD-40 or petroleum jelly and wrapped in plastic.

If you lend your tools, be sure that they are readily identifiable. Dipping tool handles in brightly colored paint makes them stand out and reminds borrowers to return them.

When sorting through your collection of nails, screws, nuts, and bolts, dispose of any fasteners that stick to a magnet. These are ferrous and subject to eventual rusting.

KNIVES   A Swiss army knife is a pocket tool of a hundred uses.

To cut line under any conditions, a serrated blade works best. Give your favorite knife a sharp serrated edge with a coarse metal file.

Another multipurpose tool is the old-fashioned marlin-spike knife, always at your side in its sheath.

SCREWDRIVER FID   A screwdriver tip can be filed down to a flattened end with rounded edges to serve as a wire-splicing fid.

SCREWDRIVER SET   A screwdriver set containing various blades that fit interchangeably into a single handle can replace many individual screwdrivers.

RAZOR BLADES   Razor blades are extremely helpful on the boat. You can keep them safely in matchbook covers.

WIRE STRIPPERS   Wire strippers can be used both to cut wire and to crimp and cut small machine screws to a proper length.

MAGNET   Use the large 50 lb. strength magnet normally used to pick up ferrous objects that have fallen over the side, to retrieve tools dropped under or behind the engine.

MIRROR   Keep a small mirror in the tool box to help you see around corners or behind the engine where space is too cramped to see properly.

How about using a dentist's mouth mirror for these hard-to-see spots?

FIBER OPTIC FLASHLIGHT   To illuminate inaccessible areas inside your engine or in dark corners of the boat, get an inexpensive fiber optic inspector's flashlight. They have long bendable optic fibers that can be cut or shaped to fit any recess. Light is emitted from the end of the fiber only.

ADJUSTABLE WRENCH   One adjustable wrench will replace a whole metric and SAE wrench set.

ALLEN WRENCHES   Rather than trying to keep loose Allen wrenches in their plastic packets, get a set that swivels on a single pin.

MEASURING TAPE   Purchase a ruler with self-sticking tape on the back. Press a short piece on the tool box for quick measurements and a longer piece near the workbench area.

DIFFICULT MEASUREMENTS   A ruler will not work to measure irregularly shaped or hard-to-reach areas. Use a long piece of string to mark the length, then measure the string.

PLIERS   Wrap plier jaws with plastic tape to avoid marring wood and plastic surfaces. Insulate plier handles with electrical tape or PVC dipping compound.

WORKBENCH   Every boat needs a workbench for the hundreds of jobs that can be done only on board. Make a

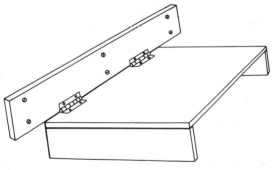

FIGURE 12

foldaway workbench that will hang flush against a bulkhead. Use an 18-inch-deep particle board as the top, and attach it to the bulkhead with hinges. Add swinging side supports at the ends. These will fold down against the bulkhead to firmly brace the workbench (see Figure 12).

VISE   It is difficult to find a place to put a vise on a sailboat. For large jobs, bolt your vise to a piece of plywood and attach the plywood to a companionway step with C clamps (see Figure 13).

For small jobs use rubber bands around plier handles to turn pliers into a vise.

When gluing boards together, clamp them tightly by wrapping them with a long strip of cut inner tube.

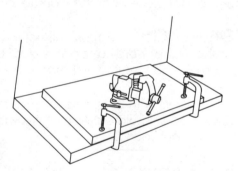

FIGURE 13

TOOL STORAGE   After spraying them with WD-40, store large tools loosely wrapped in cotton rags, then sealed in plastic bags. Keep sorted fasteners in a large-mouth, screw-top container. Keep nuts and washers on a large safety or diaper pin.

CANVAS HOLDALLS   As an alternative to the toolbox, keep tools in canvas holdalls or in shoe-bag pockets attached top and bottom to the back of a locker door. These provide excellent out-of-the-way storage (see Figure 14).

FIGURE 14

LAY-UP AND COMMISSIONING

One of the goals of this book is to predict and prevent problems before they occur. At no time is there a greater opportunity to prevent problems than at lay-up or commissioning. After you have compiled long lists of jobs to be tackled, the winter always seems too short to finish them all and only the most critical ones get done. Once you realize that almost any job is easier to do when the boat is laid up rather than in the water, you will give a higher priority to those winter projects.

HIGH-PRESSURE HOSE DOWN   After hauling, save yourself extra work by immediately hosing the boat bottom with water under high pressure to remove algae, scum, and barnacles. If it is allowed to dry, the bottom becomes much more difficult to clean.

PHOTOGRAPH BOAT IN SLING   Photograph the boat with broadside, quarter, and bow-on views when it's on the lift. This will give you a reference for strap locations for future haulouts. You could even mark the gunwale where the sling should be located next time.

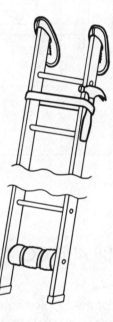

FIGURE 15

TOPSIDE PROTECTION   Protect the topside from ladder scuffs by putting an old pair of sneakers on the top ends of the ladder (see Figure 15).

Tape around the bottom rung of the ladder a cloth on which you can wipe off your muddy feet.

Put a tight piece of inner tube around the top rung of the ladder to hold extra tools while you work.

READING HULL MOISTURE   When you buy a new or used boat, it's a good time to have a surveyor check the fiberglass hull for moisture content. This will give you a reference point to compare future readings and will ease your concern about possible blisters.

WINTER COVER   In most northern climates, a breathing winter cover for a hauled boat saves a great amount of spring re-work. Lightweight PVC tubing can make an excellent, inexpensive winter cover frame.

PREVENTING CONDENSATION   By keeping a 100-watt light bulb burning below deck at all times, you can keep the temperature 1 or 2 degrees above the dewpoint and prevent harmful condensation.

At lay-up, place a few boxes of cat litter around the inside of the cabin to soak up excess moisture and odors.

VENTILATION HATCHBOARD   You can obtain excellent winter ventilation below by switching the normal hatchboard for one made of exterior plywood with dozens of holes drilled into it. Good air circulation will prevent most mildew from occurring below.

KEEPING PARTS IN ORDER   As you disassemble a pump, stove, or winch for cleaning and repair, place all those small parts on a long piece of sticky tape in the order in which they are removed.

WATER SYSTEM LAY-UP   If you choose not to drain the water system, add potable antifreeze, as the water pump manufacturer recommends. At commissioning time, flush and fill the water tank. Flush and fill again. Then add a small amount of baking soda to remove any residual antifreeze taste.

ICEBOX LAY-UP   After cleaning the icebox thoroughly, leave its lid open to keep the box fresh over the winter.

BILGE OIL CLEANUP   After pumping the bilge as dry as possible, soak up any remaining oil with disposable diapers.

ELECTROLYSIS   At haulout, inspect the zinc anodes to determine if they need replacing. Strike all through-the-hull fittings and other metal parts with a hammer to confirm that they are sound. Deteriorated bronze will usually be a splotchy pink color and produce a dull sound when struck.

FIGURE 16

Another test of metal fitness is to ground a wire to the engine and lead it over the side near the metal part in question. Touch the end of the wire to an ohmmeter that is in contact with the metal part. A reading of more than 1 ohm signals that the part may be deteriorated and should be examined carefully (see Figure 16).

This is a good time to ground the through-the-hull fittings to the boat's main grounding system to help prevent future electrolysis.

WAXING THE HULL   Many boat owners suggest waxing the hull in the fall and leaving it unpolished until spring. This can give the hull added winter protection and makes it ready for a quick polish at commissioning time.

PAINTING THE HULL IN SPRING   When painting the hull on the cradle, remove the supporting pads one at a time. Paint beneath each one. When the paint is dry, put wax paper under the pad and return it to its original place.

PROTECTING ENGINE INTAKE

Dip a rag in a can of bottom paint, and jam it into the engine intake pipe. The antifouling paint will protect the pipe from marine growth.

WINTERIZING THE WINCH

After dismantling, washing, greasing, and reassembling winches, leave their cloth covers on during the winter.

NONSKID SURFACES

Three of the best nonskid surfaces are a teak inlay, a nonskid overlay, and nonskid paint. Apply any one of these to floorboards, ladders, bowsprit, companionway steps, or boarding areas.

Casting sand or polymer beads make excellent grit to sprinkle into paint to create a nonskid area.

There is even the technique of adding epsom salts to paint, then washing the paint after it dries. The epsom salts dissolve, leaving a pitted nonskid surface.

RENEWING NONSKID SURFACE

To repair a worn area on a factory molded, nonskid deck, you will have to match the surface pattern. To accomplish this, spray release agent on an area of nonskid surface that is in good condition, put down a layer of silicone sealant, and peel it off when it has cured. Apply polyester resin to the worn-out area. Now press the silicone mold, previously sprayed with release agent, into the uncured polyester resin to duplicate the pattern. Remove the mold after the resin has cured, and paint the entire nonskid area.

REFURBISHING TEAK

Don't use stiff brushes on teak decks because the hard bristles will dig out the softer wood, leaving grooved teak.

Clean teak with salt water, soap, and a soft scrubber. Because the salt holds moisture, it will help to swell small dents and keep the teak from drying out.

PROTECTING RUBBER

Sprayed petroleum lubricants will damage rubber. When applying these lubricants, carefully protect rubber and Neoprene bedding compounds and gaskets.

CLEANING MAST AND STAYS   When the aluminum mast is on the ground for inspection during lay-up, clean it with detergent, going after the worst stains with bronze wool.

CARE OF RIGGING   After cleaning spars with bronze wool, carefully inspect them with a magnifying glass for cracks. Lubricate moving parts with lanolin. Inspect all shrouds for meathooks, and put penetrating oil on terminal fittings.

STORING SPARS   Don't store spars in tightly wrapped plastic. They need air to prevent moisture and subsequent corrosion.

OUTBOARD LAY-UP   Allow the outboard to run completely out of fuel. At the last moment, squirt a small amount of WD-40 into the carburetor intake to prevent condensation in the engine.

INBOARD LAY-UP   The procedure of squirting WD-40 into the carburetor intake works equally well with an inboard gas engine. This is a good alternative to removing the plugs and putting oil in each cylinder.

FUEL TANK LAY-UP   Keep a diesel fuel tank full over the winter to prevent condensation. A gasoline fuel tank should be emptied because fuel that is several months old becomes inefficient.

FUEL CONDITIONER   If fuel is to be left in the tank over the winter, add a fuel storage stabilizer to further prevent problems. MDR Stor-n-Start diesel storage stabilizer or equivalent can be purchased at most marine supply stores.

SLACK DRIVE BELTS   By relieving the tension on your drive belt during storage, you can prevent stress on the bearings and belts.

HOMEMADE OIL CAN   If it is impossible to reach a hidden spot with the oil can, bend a pipe cleaner to the shape required and pour oil so that it runs down the pipe cleaner and into the target.

TAG KEYS Tag your ignition keys to remind yourself that you have closed the through-the-hulls and slackened the drive belts. This will alert you to make the necessary adjustments before you start the boat engine during commissioning in the spring.

CARE OF THE PROP Tap your propeller. A damaged prop will sound dull whereas one in good condition will ring.

Before spring commissioning, polish the prop and coat the shaft and prop with Teflon grease to prevent marine growth.

TIGHTENING PACKING NUT Some water should be allowed to enter the boat through the packing gland. By tightening or loosening the shaft packing nut, you can adjust the correct amount of leakage for proper lubrication. While the boat is on the cradle, turn the prop with the engine in neutral, and adjust to the right "feel." In the water, turn the shaft using a padded wrench to achieve the correct drip rate.

BUG BOMB A few days before commissioning the boat, set off a bug bomb in the closed cabin to get rid of any uninvited winter guests.

REPAIRS, MAINTENANCE, AND IMPROVEMENTS

Every repair job takes longer and is more difficult on the boat than at home. The lack of a good workbench, adequate storage, and large power tools makes every task harder. There are, however, many time-tested as well as a few new ideas on how to make boat repairs with the tools at hand. The information that follows will help you to improvise with materials found on board as well as to use techniques borrowed from shore-bound master carpenters, plumbers, and metal workers.

HOMEMADE HAND CLEANER   Clean grease from your hands with baking soda and water. Grease will also be easier to remove if you put on hand lotion or petroleum jelly before working on the engine.

GARBAGE BAG APRON   Cut arm and head holes in a garbage bag to use for a temporary apron when you do dirty work.

REPAIRING A STICKING DOOR   When a door sticks, it is easy to find the exact trouble spot. Put a piece of carbon paper in the door jam and close the door. The carbon left on the door will mark the spot needing sanding.

REMOVING WOOD PLUGS   To remove a wood plug, drill a small pilot hole in the plug and insert a screw. As the screw is tightened, it will back out the plug.

When replacing wood plugs, align the wood grain for a better match. Use epoxy glue if you want the plug to be permanent. Use varnish as glue if you want to remove the plug some day.

KNOT REPAIR   If the board you are working on has a knot in it, remove the knot and glue it back in with epoxy glue. This will prevent it from becoming loose with time.

WOOD DENTS   To repair a shallow dent in wood, apply a hot iron over a wet towel to the spot. The moist heat will swell the wood. In the case of a deeper dent, poking a number of holes in the wood with a fine pin or needle before the ironing procedure may improve the results.

END GRAIN FASTENING   Screws do not grab well when put into the end grain of a wooden board. To improve the hold, drill through the end of the board close enough for the screw to penetrate. Fill the hole with a piece of dowel. Now, when the screw is inserted, it will be anchored in the cross grain of the dowel (see Figure 17).

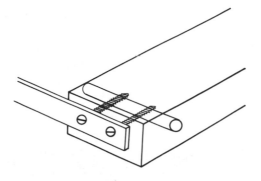

FIGURE 17

FLOORBOARD SQUEAK Try rubbing bar soap on the area where you have a squeaky floorboard to silence the squeak.

REPAIRING WITH RIVETS By using a pop rivet gun, you can fasten thin materials together with aluminum rivets and washers. Emergency joining of torn canvas, repairing broken plastic with plastic patches, and fastening small hardware to fiberglass are a few of the possible uses.

MOVING HEAVY OBJECTS To move a heavy object, drive a wedge under a corner so a lifting strap can be slid underneath.
Try using a broom to drag something too heavy to carry.

LOOSENING LOCKS To loosen a stiff lock, lubricate it with graphite. Put graphite on the key rather than in the key hole for best results.

FROZEN SCREW To loosen a frozen screw, apply penetrating oil. Rap the head hard to set up a loosening vibration and attempt to remove as usual. In the future, prevent seizing of screws by rubbing screw threads with soap, lithium machine grease, lanolin, or beeswax before inserting.

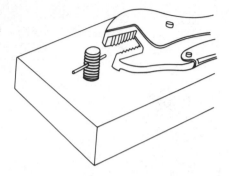

FIGURE 18

BROKEN SCREW OR BOLT HEAD   One of the most frustrating jobs is to try to remove a screw or bolt with a broken head. If there is a projection, file the edges or bang them with a punch so that a wrench can get a grip. For rounded-off heads, grasp the head with a wrench and force a screwdriver tip under one jaw of the wrench to create additional leverage.

If the end can't be grasped, drill a small hole through the exposed shank. Insert a pin in the hole and grip it with a wrench (see Figure 18).

If the screw is broken flush, use a screw extractor. Tap the extractor into a hole drilled in the top of the screw. Back it out by tightening and turning a wrench on the extractor. As a last resort, you can drill out the entire screw or bolt.

DUNKED OUTBOARD   If an outboard is dunked in salt water while the engine is running, corrosion will occur. Immediately immerse the engine in fresh water. Take it to the repair shop as soon as possible.

BATTERY CLEANER   A clean battery top prevents unnecessary electrical leakage. To clean, plug the vent holes with toothpicks and scrub the top with baking soda and water. Rinse the top, and then remove the toothpicks.

Auto parts stores sell impregnated felt washers that fit over the battery terminals to prevent corrosion.

FROZEN NUT   Drill a diagonal hole through a rusted frozen nut to expose threads to penetrating oil.

Use a hand-driven impact wrench that fits over the nut. A hard rap on the Impact wrench will loosen the nut.

Try a nutcracker that splits the nut and allows its removal.

Tightening rather than attempting to loosen the nut will often break it loose.

If you heat the nut with a torch or soldering iron, the nut will sometimes expand and come loose.

BROKEN ALLEN SCREW   You can often remove a damaged Allen screw by hammering a screwdriver into the recess, then turning the screwdriver with a wrench.

STRIPPED THREAD REPAIR   Smear epoxy putty on stripped threads and tighten the nut. This is permanent and should be done only as a last resort.

Rusted threads can be carefully cleaned with a small triangular metal file.

FIGURE 19

CUTTING PLASTIC SHEET   When cutting plastic sheet, score it first, put a piece of dowel under the score line, and then snap the sheet down using both hands (see Figure 19).

CUTTING PLASTIC PIPE   A hacksaw is the best tool for cutting plastic pipe.

CUTTING WIRE   When using wire cutters, an abrupt snap cuts better than a scissor cut.

CUTTING METAL PIPE   Put a stainless steel hose clamp at the place to be cut. Scribe a line along the clamp's edge to create a straight cutting guide.

CUTTING METAL   After putting the metal piece in a vise, start the cut with short forward strokes of the hacksaw. Use your thumb as a guide. Apply very little pressure on the back stroke to make it as easy as possible.

POWER DRILLING   When drilling metal, first mark the entry spot with a center punch. Start slowly and gradually increase the speed, keeping the pressure even. Back the drill out often, with motor running, to clear chips and cool the drill bit.

DRILL LUBRICANTS   When cutting aluminum, use kerosene as a lubricant. For mild steel use a light oil. For stainless steel, use a commercial drilling compound.

HAND DRILLS   In this age of electrical gadgets, don't forget the crank-operated hand drill, which works like a charm. If you drill into plastic, be sure to back it with a piece of wood, to reinforce the plastic and keep it from cracking.

CORDLESS POWER TOOLS   Most of the new cordless power tools will operate for at least one hour before needing a recharge. Keeping a charged second battery allows you to work without stopping.

   If you are doing work while at sea, cordless drills with high-speed bits make any job a great deal easier.

STARTING SCREWS   To insert a screw in a spot that is difficult to reach, push the screw through a piece of masking tape, sticky side up, and position the screwdriver in the screw slot. Press the tape to both sides of the screwdriver. This will hold the screw until it bites (see Figure 20).

FIGURE 20

RESEALING CAULKING GUN After using a caulking gun, put a machine screw in the nozzle to keep the contents from drying.

SPARK PLUG REMOVER Remove a difficult-to-reach spark plug by putting a socket over the plug and then twisting the socket with locking pliers.

EXHAUST PIPE REPAIR A leaking exhaust pipe can be temporarily repaired with a muffler and tailpipe bandage. These can be purchased from a local truckstop. The bandage consists of a two-part tape containing epoxy resin. Clean the damaged area with a wire brush, apply tape, and run the engine until the pipe is hot. The high temperature welds the tape to the exhaust pipe.

BROKEN FAN BELT If you do not have a spare fan belt, loop a line around the pulleys, securing the ends with a knot. Tighten the movable pulley and start the engine. Install a new fan belt at the first opportunity.

ENGINE OIL LEAKS Put a pan under an engine oil leak to catch the oil. Pour the collected oil back into the engine as often as necessary until you reach your destination.

ENLARGED SCREW HOLES

When replacing a screw in an existing hole, use a larger screw rather than reusing the original. If you must use the same screw, fill the hole with toothpicks so that the screw has new wood to enter.

RIGGING REPAIR

To join a wire to a terminal fitting in an emergency, you can improvise a Nicropress tool. Hold the Nicropress fitting with a vise grip against a large metal tool. Carefully tap a screwdriver into the groove of the fitting to close it. Replace this temporary repair at the first opportunity.

QUALITY LOCKNUTS

Because single and even double nuts tend to vibrate loose, try using nylon insert locknuts. They have been found to be very reliable by the aircraft industry.

METAL REPAIR

You can repair small leaks in metal tanks by screwing a self-taping screw into the hole causing the leak.

SPARE METAL PARTS

Many problems at sea can be corrected if you have a good inventory of spare metal materials.

Sheets of aluminum can easily be cut and pounded to a specific shape.

Precut shrouds can be a lifesaver when needed.

Copper pipe is very easy to cut and has many possible uses.

No. 302 annealed stainless wire is very soft and can be twisted to tie innumerable objects together.

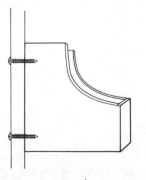

FIGURE 21

HANGING RACKS ON BULKHEAD   To achieve the greatest holding strength when hanging a heavy object, attach the object to the bulkhead with screws inserted from behind, rather than into the visible side of the bulkhead (see Figure 21).

PLASTIC REPAIRS   Cracks or splits often develop in acrylic at the site of a screw. To reinforce the weakened area, remove the screw and drill the hole a little larger. Replace the screw by inserting one with a larger head.

ALUMINUM REPAIR   To remove small dents from aluminum sheet, back the dent with a wood block and strike the dent with a rubber hammer. Wrap a metal hammer with insulating material if you do not have a rubber one on board.

Patch small holes in aluminum with epoxy putty. Use a scrap aluminum piece behind the hole to hold the putty in place.

CAST IRON REPAIR   To temporarily repair a broken piece of cast iron, clean the edges with steel wool and join with epoxy glue.

PIPE REPAIR   Almost any pipe or hose can be temporarily repaired by fitting a rubber gasket over the hole and holding it tight with a few stainless steel hose clamps.

TWO-PART PUTTYS   Methyl ethyl ketone is the usual cleaning and drying solvent of choice used to prepare a surface for application of a two-part putty. A minimum temperature is required to cure any two-part putty. If you must work below the manufacturer's recommended temperature, however, use a hair drier to raise the temperature of the uncured resin.

REPLACING FROZEN SEACOCK   The easiest time to replace a frozen seacock is when the boat is out of the water. Use a protecting block of wood to lightly hammer out a corroded seacock.

If the boat is in the water, go over the side and plug the through-the-hull fitting. Return to the boat and remove the seacock as above. Install the repaired seacock, get back in the water, and remove the plug.

To repair a corroded seacock, soak it in penetrating oil to separate the parts. Coat the threads with an abrasive, and twist the seacock back and forth in its shell to clean out the threads. Clean, rinse, lubricate, and reinstall.

FIBERGLASS SCRATCHES

FIBERGLASS SCRATCHES Shoe polish is made of high-quality pigment and wax. Why not use it for scratch repair on dark hulls? For larger gel coat repairs, tape a piece of plastic film over the uncured gel coat to give it a smooth surface.

UNDERWATER REPAIRS

UNDERWATER REPAIRS When you have to go underwater to check the prop or do other repairs, snug a taut line around the hull to hold onto while you work below (see Figure 22).

The underwater work will be easier if you wear a face mask and gloves and tie the tools to your arm with a lanyard.

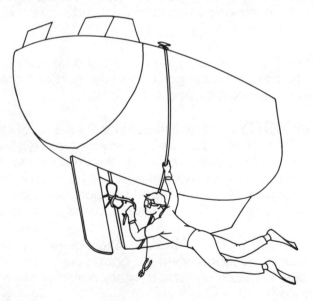

FIGURE 22

EPOXY PUTTY STICKS   You can now purchase epoxy putty that comes in two chewing gum-like sticks. Kneading the two together in your hands activates the two-part putty. It is tough and ideal for underwater patches.

VELCRO   Then there is the indispensable Velcro. Attach strips to pens, flashlights, tools, galley utensils or any small object to be hung. Use it on the bottom of your coffee cup, to gather wiring, or to make better seals on your old foul-weather gear.

SOLDER REPAIR   Silver solder due to its low melt point does not require a special soldering iron to apply. By heating stainless steel, brass, copper, or bronze fittings over a flame, silver solder can be directly applied to easily mend a crack.

DISPOSABLE RUBBER GLOVES   Prepowdered disposable rubber gloves, sold at drug stores, can afford excellent hand protection from solvents, glues, resins, paints, and stains. Be sure to check package labeling regarding the gloves' resistance to specific chemicals.

To remove heavier rubber gloves from your hands more easily, first run them under cold water.

THE INS AND OUTS OF CLEANING

There are hundreds of cleaning preparations on the market that will do most of the jobs called for on a boat. They are quite specific and well known. Consumers usually develop a preference for one product or another. There are, however, some homemade cleaning compounds that can salvage stained clothing or clean metal when your favorite commercial product runs out. Common sense dictates that before using any cleaning preparation, commercial or homemade, you try it in a hidden corner to determine its compatibility with the substrate to be cleaned.

MILDEWED ENAMEL   Clean mildew from enamel surfaces in the cabin with a mixture of turpentine and bleach. The paint surface will resist further mildew growth after it dries.

VARNISH CLEANER   Mix 20 percent vinegar and water to clean varnish.

WOODWORK BELOW DECK   Wood trim that is below deck, unlike unvarnished woodwork above deck, can be treated as household furniture. Frequent rubdowns with lemon oil furniture polish are advisable.

CLEANING CLOTH   Put a cotton gym sock on your hand to apply metal cleaner.

CLEANING IN TIGHT SPOTS   Specialty hardware stores and catalogs carry brass or stainless steel brushes the size of a toothbrush. Use them to remove rust, corrosion, and dirt in tight spots. They also help to clean saws, drills, and other tools. The brass or stainless steel bristles will not damage machine surfaces, cutting edges, or solder.

A fine-bristle rat-tail brush will get into corners and edges for final clean up before painting.

CLEANING BRASS   An old method of cleaning brass used by the British navy is to rub the stained metal with a lemon dipped in salt.

Another method is to rub stained brass with full-strength ammonia and fine steel wool. Rinse thoroughly, and apply brass polish.

POLISHING BRASS BAROMETER   To prevent metal polish stains on the bulkhead when you clean a mounted barometer, slip a cardboard template over the barometer or cover the surrounding area with masking tape.

POLISHING BRONZE   To polish bronze, use a salt and vinegar solution or a strong detergent applied with fine bronze wool.

Let teak oil remain on stained bronze for a few minutes; then rinse and polish.

CLEANING STAINLESS STEEL Stainless steel in the galley and head can be kept sparkling clean by using window cleaner or ammonia applied with paper towels.

POLISHING CHROME Wipe clean chrome with a very light application of WD-40 to keep it looking bright.

CLEANING BARBECUE Keep a small brass bristle brush handy to scrape and clean a chrome barbeque. It will not scratch, yet is stiff enough to remove most baked-on grime.

CLEANING SCREENS Clean screens with kerosene and nylon mesh; then rinse with detergent and water.

CLEANING THE HULL The tannic acid and grime at the water line leave a yellow stain on the hull that can easily be removed with a solution of oxalic acid. As always, be very careful when handling oxalic acid and, preferably, wear gloves. Wax the hull after rinsing.

STAINS ON A FIBERGLASS DECK To remove small spots and stains from the fiberglass deck, apply floor wax remover, rinse, and reapply wax.

CLEANING PVC Harsh abrasives pit PVC and cause subsequent staining to occur more rapidly. Use a soft scrub household cleaner or floor wax cleaner. Mineral spirits may also be used, but they must be removed at once. Regardless of which compound you use, rinse away the cleaning agent and protect the surface with a coat of wax.

CLEANING GLASS Clean glass with a solution of hot water and a small amount of kerosene. Apply with a well-wrung-out clean cloth. The fine film of kerosene will keep the glass clean longer.

CLEANING THE HEAD Put a small amount of chlorine bleach in a flush-pump type head a few times each season to keep it smelling fresh.

ALL-PURPOSE BOAT CLEANER Local paint stores carry a water-soluble brush cleaner that will clean grease, oil, un-cured resin, glue, tar, and creosote as well as brushes. Be sure to keep it away from plastics, paint, and varnish.

CLEANING CLOTHS A nearly universal cleaning material is nylon mesh. Use it freely because it will not scratch any surface and can be easily cleaned.

Highly absorbent heavy terry cloth works well as a clean-ing, drying, or polishing cloth.

Specially impregnated cotton fleece for polishing metal is available. However, clean, soft cotton from a variety of sources does an almost equal job.

DISPOSABLE DIAPERS Unlimited uses for disposable di-apers come to mind. Few materials are as absorbent when you are cleaning spills, soaking up oil under the engine, dry-ing the bilge, polishing and buffing. Cloth diapers are excel-lent, too, but are not as readily disposable.

SCRUBBING PADS Plastic dishwashing pads do a great job for final cleaning of the boat bottom. Brillo pads are excellent for cleaning the prop.

PAINTING: SHIPSHAPE AND BRISTOL FASHION

Now we enter the domain of real choice. There are hundreds of paint products and dozens of companies that offer coatings for the marine environment. Most marine finishes are best ap-plied by a professional painter. All paint companies now real-ize that sailors are the ultimate do-it-yourselfers, however. Tinkering and fixing are literally part of their license to sail. Therefore, there is an ample array of paint products available to the amateur that, if applied with proper technique, give excellent results.

PAINT STORAGE One of the greatest fire hazards on a boat or at home is the forgotten cache of flammable liquids. If you must keep paints, solvents, and teak oils on the boat, store them in a deck locker, not below.

PETROLEUM JELLY PROTECTION Instead of removing all the hardware from an area to be painted, coat all metal parts with petroleum jelly. This prevents paint from sticking to hardware.

REVIVE OLD PAINT In time, pigment settles to the bottom in cans of paint. These old paints can be brought back to use by careful stirring. Insert a beater from a household electric mixer into a power drill and stir at low drill speed (see Figure 23).

FIGURE 23

WHITER WHITE By adding a small amount of blue tinting color to your white paint, you can diminish the inevitable yellowing that most white enamels develop when exposed to sunlight.

ROLLER/BRUSH URETHANE FINISHES Spray application of urethane provides an excellent, smooth finish. It is possible to approach this quality by using good roller and brush techniques however. After very careful preparation, apply the urethane with the roller and immediately crosscut with a brush to an extremely smooth finish. Buff with wet sandpaper after each coat. Before applying the last coat, evaluate the finish. You may decide to put down a roller/brush top coat or to have a final coat sprayed on professionally.

CLEAN RIM OF CAN   It is nearly impossible to get wet paint out of the rim of the can. To prevent this paint from splashing, be sure to cover the can lid with a cloth when you pound the lid closed.

To minimize the unwanted collection of paint, poke a few holes in the rim of the can with an icepick to allow the wet paint to drain back into the can.

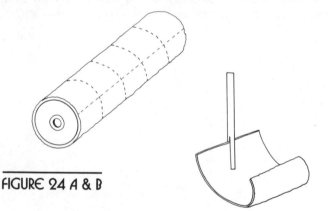

FIGURE 24 A & B

EPOXY APPLICATOR   Because epoxy hardens very quickly, it is far more convenient to use disposable applicators. Split a conventional paint roller lengthwise, and cross section each half into five pieces (see Figure 24A). Jam a section into the split end of a stick, and use it to apply the epoxy (see Figure 24B). When the pad begins to get stiff, throw it away and insert another piece.

QUALITY BRUSHES   To select a high-quality brush, look for one that has split ends on most of its bristles.

TRIM ROLLER EDGES If you are getting thick paint lines at the outer edges of the roller, trim the roller cloth edges slightly with scissors.

TEMPORARY BRUSH STORAGE If you must put a brush or roller down for a lengthy rest break, put it in a plastic bag to keep it wet.

An enamel brush can be kept wet longer by suspending it in a coffee can half full of thinner. Cut a hole in the plastic lid of the coffee can. Poke the brush handle through the lid to hold the bristles just off the bottom of the can. The bristles will stay wet and not become permanently bent over (see Figure 25).

FIGURE 25

CLEANING PAINT ROLLERS An easier way to clean a roller is to put it in a solvent-filled tennis ball can or similar container and shake.

CLEANING BRUSHES To clean paint brushes, rinse them with thinner and shake dry in a paper bag. Wash brushes thoroughly in detergent and water, rinse, comb out the bristles, and store wrapped in newspaper.

Another technique for cleaning a brush requires rinsing it in kerosene, dipping it in engine oil, and wrapping it in plastic or foil. Rinse out the brush in kerosene before using it again.

CLEANING VARNISH BRUSH
Best results will always be obtained by using a new, high-quality varnish brush. If it is well cared for, however, an old brush can give excellent performance.

To clean a varnish brush, rinse often in thinner and shake dry. Wrap it in newspaper to maintain its shape. Then hang it in a can of thinner, supported so that the bristles don't touch the bottom. Rinse in clean thinner before its next use.

VARNISH
Purchase varnish that contains UV protector to extend its outdoor life.

VARNISH TACK CLOTH
Make onetime varnish tack rags from clean 100 percent cotton T-shirts or cheesecloth. Soak rags in varnish solvent or turpentine. Pour about a tablespoon of varnish on the rag, and wring it out very well. Allow the rag to become partially dry before using it.

VARNISHING TECHNIQUES
Cleanliness is the essential ingredient in a good varnish job. Sand, vacuum, and wipe the surface with a tack cloth to prepare it for varnishing.

To lessen the chance of bubbles, use fresh varnish that has not been stirred or shaken. Keep fresh varnish in one clean, shallow can. Pat excess varnish off the brush into a second can.

When you apply varnish, first brush along the grain. Follow with an across-the-grain stroke with more varnish. Finally, smooth in the original direction with an almost dry brush. Don't overwork the wet area. Stroke toward the edge, lifting the brush before going over. Stroke varnish away from, rather than into, a corner.

Sanding and thorough cleaning with a tack rag are essential before each coat of varnish is applied. For the final coat, consider taking the boat to sea on a clear, sunny day. Dust-free air will be your reward.

Don't apply wax to a varnished surface. The wax will prevent varnish from adhering the next time you apply a touch-up coat.

VARNISH TOUCH-UP KIT
Varnish can be kept handy in a clean paste jar, such as is used in grade schools, to perform

small touch-up jobs. The paste brush in the lid can adequately apply enough varnish to repair a small scratch.

DRY HULL   If you are not sure the hull is dry enough to paint, tape and seal clear plastic sheets over a few small areas on the hull. If the areas under the plastic are free of condensation after twenty-four hours, the hull is ready for painting.

CLEANING OFF SILICONE WAX   A mixture of equal parts turpentine and a powder detergent is effective for removal of silicone wax. However, this mixture will harm paint surfaces if left on for any length of time. Therefore, clean a small area at a time, rinsing promptly. If surface water still beads, there is residual silicone present, and the procedure should be repeated.

POWER SANDER   Save time by loading the sander with a few layers of sandpaper. As the paper becomes fouled with paint, tear the top one off exposing a fresh sheet.

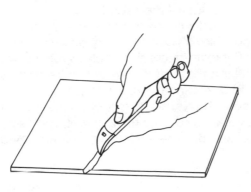

FIGURE 26

REPAIRING CRACKS   To repair small cracks in wood or fiberglass, the fissure must be widened before it can be filled. Use the sharp end of a beer can opener to cut a V-groove in a crack to get better filler adhesion (see Figure 26).

SANDING STEEL WOOL   Bronze wool works better than steel wool for fine sanding wood before varnishing. Steel wool leaves small pieces of steel in the surface that will rust and ruin the look of the varnish.

SANDING TECHNIQUES
Always sand in the same direction on fiberglass and with the grain on wood.

Using heavy pressure and fine paper is not as satisfactory as using coarser paper with light pressure.

Sand the boat bottom with very coarse, wet sandpaper. Wet sanding is faster and not as dusty as dry sanding, but it is still as messy a job as you can find.

SANDING FIBERGLASS
Fiberglass dust is very irritating to the skin and should never be inhaled. Irritation and itch can be reduced if you apply lotion to exposed skin areas, cover your mouth and nose with a respirator, and wear gloves when sanding fiberglass.

MASKING TAPE
To prevent paint from seeping under the masking tape and onto protected areas, press the tape firmly against the hull. You can do this by rubbing a tool handle along the paint edge of the masking tape.

When you have finished the painting, remove the tape as soon as possible. It becomes very difficult to get the masking tape and glue residue off the hull if it remains on too long. Peel the masking tape off in the same direction as it was applied to avoid disturbing any undried paint.

If you don't have masking tape, substitute strips of wet newspaper. As long as they remain wet, they will stick to almost any surface. Be sure to remove before they get too dry.

HULL STRIPES
The easiest way to paint a decorative stripe on the hull is to use a stencil. Buy the widest available car racing stripe at an auto supply store. These normally come in a roll composed of eight $1/16$-inch peel-off stripes. Apply the entire tape to the hull, and remove as many of the middle stripes as needed to expose the desired width. Use the exposed area as a template, and paint a perfectly even stripe.

BOAT LETTERING
Lettering is not easy, but with a little preparation and care, it can be accomplished by an amateur.

Draw the letters on the pattern found on the reverse side of contact paper. Transfer these letters to tracing paper and darken the back side of the tracing paper with black chalk. Center and tape the tracing paper to the hull. Trace the letters with a pencil, leaving a chalk imprint on the hull. Use a high-quality enamel and brush for painting. Now all you need is a steady hand and a sunny day.

CHAPTER 3

BELOW DECK

Below deck areas are not critical to the safe and efficient movement of the boat. However, a well-run galley, dry and ample storage, and a clean and efficient head can vastly improve the quality of sailing life.

THE CABIN: HOME AWAY FROM HOME

After years of design improvements, the cabin is a compact and efficient space. However, additional adjustments can make it possible to avoid unnecessary clutter, make safer working conditions, and provide more living comfort.

ACRYLIC COMPANIONWAY BOARDS To improve the light below, replace companionway boards with tinted acrylic sheets. Select acrylic slightly thinner than the present wood pieces to allow for thermal expansion. Cut these to shape with a very fine power saw blade.

GULL-WINGED STEPS If the boat is tender and often heeled, changing the companionway steps to a gull-winged shape makes going up and down much easier (see Figure 27).

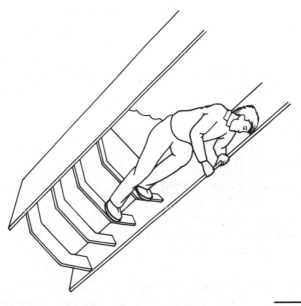

FIGURE 27

STORAGE OF COILED LINE   Install a small rack with pegs behind the companionway steps. It's a perfect out-of-the-way yet handy location to hang coiled docking lines and sail stops.

WOOD GRATING AS CABIN SOLE   Replace a small part of the wood floorboard at the bottom of the companionway with wood grating. Water brought below will drain into the bilge and not make the carpet or floorboards wet.

SECURE DINETTE   All items below should be made secure in rough weather. The dinette is no exception but is often overlooked. To keep it from coming loose, attach a lifting ring to the cabin sole and a pelican hook under the table at a proper distance to reach the lifting ring. When connected, these will keep the dinette very secure.

DINETTE SUPPORTS   Better support for the drop leaves of a dinette is obtained with spring hatch hinges. The spring is bent when the drop leaf is down. Straightening the spring locks the leaf in the extended position.

FIGURE 28

TOO TIGHT FLOORBOARDS Too often floorboards don't have enough space between them, making them very difficult to remove. Taper the edges of the boards to make the crack wider at the bottom than at the top (see Figure 28). This technique maintains the same tight fitting look while preventing the boards from sticking.

CLEANING FRESHWATER PLASTIC TUBING Algae grow easily in clear plastic tubing. To reduce the frequency of cleaning, replace the clear tubing with an opaque variety. Because light does not penetrate opaque tubing, algae will not grow as readily.

When it is necessary to clean tubing, attach a swab dipped in bleach to a string and pull it through the tube.

REARRANGING WEIGHT DISTRIBUTION Lowering the boat's center of gravity improves its stability. This can be accomplished by placing weight as low in the boat as possible. For example, remove the life raft from the deck; lead the anchor and chain lower and further aft; and, place canned goods and books midship.

EXTRA FLOTATION Air trapped in fuel and water tanks, cushions and mattresses or other buoyant items on board gives boats a great deal of added flotation. However, extra flotation can be added, preferably with the advice of a naval architect who will probably recommend that spaces be filled with poured foam or Styrofoam blocks over the full length of the boat and as low as possible.

WATER BALLAST   An idea gaining acceptance is to use water as ballast. Install starboard and port tanks that can be selectively filled with water. Sailing trim on long beats can be radically improved by using this technique.

FIRE EXTINGUISHER HOLDER   An inexpensive fire extinguisher holder can be easily fabricated from a short piece of PVC pipe attached to the cabin bulkhead. Drill holes in the bottom end cap to allow drainage.

INFLATABLE MATTRESS   Extra beds can be provided by using inflatable twin-size mattresses. Get the variety with large air filling holes that can be quickly inflated with a hair dryer on the cold setting. The hair dryer can also be used to fill inflatable toys and floats.

Placing a mattress on the cabin sole makes a padded confined area for very small children.

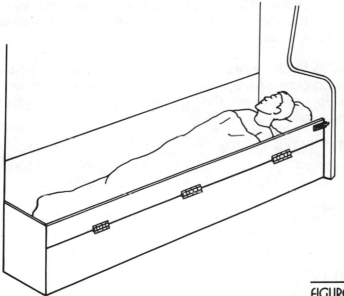

FIGURE 29

LEE BOARDS   Provide extra storage space and safer sleeping conditions by using bunk lee boards. Using hinges, connect a lee board to the outer edge of a bunk. Barrel bolts should be installed on the bulkhead to secure the board in its upright position (see Figure 29).

LAYERED SLEEPING BAG   It is common knowledge that layering clothing provides the most warmth and allows you to peel off layers to optimize comfort. Why not fabricate a multi-layer sleeping bag using the same principle? Construct a zippered bag with removable layers: first a sheet; then a light cotton blanket; next, a synthetic cold-weather layer; and last, a tough waterproof shell. By adjusting the layers of this special sleeping bag, you can compensate for dramatic temperature shifts.

LARGER V-BERTHS   Cushion and cover a V-berth insert to expand the forward sleeping area. Hang the insert on bulkhead hooks during the day.

V-BERTH CONTOUR SHEETS   Cut a king-size sheet to the V-berth shape with 6 to 10 extra inches all around. Sew elastic at the corners to create a fitted bottom sheet.

FOLDING STEP   Install a folding bronze step on the V-berth bulkhead beneath the overhead hatch to provide improved access for climbing out through the hatch or to assist you in getting a sailbag out on deck.

INSTANT BED WARMER   Flannel sheets are remarkable for their warmth. On warm nights they can be used as light blankets. Each washing makes them feel better and softer.

DAYTIME SLEEP   Sleep will come more easily if the crew off watch use ear plugs and eye masks to keep out the noise and light.

NIGHT LIGHTS   To protect the night vision of the crew when they go below, use a red light in the galley.
 A few coats of red Magic Marker or nail polish will give a red glow to a conventional light bulb.
 Keep a flashlight near your bunk at night.

BUG PROTECTION   There are bugproof mesh bunk enclosures that set up in seconds to protect you from noisy biting insects. They can be found in camping or sporting goods stores.

Plastic mesh screens attached to ports and hatches with Velcro will help to keep pests out of the cabin. Repair small holes in the porthole or hatch cover screens by pushing the strands back in place with an icepick.

Old-fashioned punk sticks are a simple and effective way to repel flying insects. Support a lighted punk in a glass on the dinette. Its pleasant smoke will chase bugs away for at least an hour.

VELCRO IDEAS   Put Velcro on the bottom of electronics to keep them in place. Use Velcro to hang pictures on the bulkhead. Velcro loops are effective for hanging items in lazarets or lockers. These loops are also useful in the cabin to hold cups, binoculars, and flashlights.

MINIHAMMOCK   Hang a small hammock over each bunk to hold keys, wallets, books, flashlight, and eyeglasses.

NETTING BELOW   Netting is normally used only on the foredeck to keep sails and children on board. It can also be used stretched across the V-berth entrance to make a child's playpen or for safe storage.

Stretching netting taut against the forward bulkhead can provide safe, out-of-the-way storage for boathooks, oars, and fishing poles.

DOUBLE ANCHOR LOCKER   It can be very convenient to have separate chain lockers for the occasion when setting two anchors is wise. By fabricating a divider in the center of the existing locker, two chains and anchors can be stored below without fear of tangling. Be certain to have drain holes in each section.

COCKROACH CONTROL   Do everything you can to prevent bringing cockroaches on board. Don't bring supplies on the boat with paper bags or cardboard boxes. Leave nonperishables on the dock in the hot sun to drive any potential boarders away.

   Scatter boric acid carefully throughout the boat to eliminate any critters already present. Remember that boric acid can be poisonous to children and pets if it is consumed in large doses, so be sure to place it out of the way. As an alternative, use diatomaceous earth, commonly used for swimming pool filtration. Cement powder mixed with sugar will also kill the pests.

MOUSE REMOVAL   Occasionally, larger boats are bothered with mice. They seem to like peanut butter better than cheese for trap bait. Mice also will not live around the smell of mint.

SHIP'S NOTEBOOK   An invaluable help to owner, crew, and guests is a detailed, three-ring ship's notebook. It should tell where all equipment and supplies are located. It should also include procedures on radio operation, specifics on haulout, and compass deviation information. Manuals can be placed in the back for quick reference. In this way, all information pertaining to boat operation will be found in one readily accessible spot.

HYDROPONICS   Conditions in the cabin are nearly perfect for hydroponically growing lettuce, tomatoes, spinach, strawberries, herbs, and flowers. Hydroponics is the science of growing plants in water, without soil, in an inert, nonorganic medium that is saturated regularly with prepared nutrients. A number of books have been written about hydroponic gardening. Designs are available for the inexpensive construction of long, hanging "socks" to contain the growing medium, nutrients, and plants.

NAVIGATIONAL WRISTWATCH   Most navigational functions can be performed on scientific digital watches. Formulas for solving navigational sight problems can be scratched on the rear face of the watch for quick reference.

GIMBALED CHART TABLE   Put the chart table on gimbals to make the navigator more comfortable when working on a severely heeled boat.
  Keep a magnifying glass in the chart table drawer.

ENDLESS NOTE PAPER   Mount a roll of adding machine tape near the navigation table for handy note taking and calculations.

CHART CARE   Reinforce the fold lines of well-used charts by putting wide transparent tape on the reverse side.

CHART TABLE   If you sail frequently in the same area, glue the local chart to the navigation table top and overcoat with a few layers of clear urethane varnish.
  Or clip a clear acrylic sheet to the table top so that a chart can be slipped under the plastic sheet.
  Both of these ideas keep a frequently used chart handy. They also allow you to mark on the plastic surface repeatedly without ruining the chart with erasures.

PHOTOGRAPH RECORDS   Keep a file of all your boat records and personal documents on 35-millimeter black and white negatives. These negatives will take very little space and always be accessible. Keep them dry in Ziploc bags with a written contents list enclosed. Should there be a theft, these negatives would help prove ownership for insurance purposes.
  Seldom used large-scale charts can be photographed in the same manner. With the aid of a magnifying glass, these negatives can be read with surprising clarity.

STORAGE OF LAMP FUEL   Small plastic squeeze bottles filled with kerosene make refilling lamps in rough weather less messy.

RUG FOR CABIN SOLE   To have a warm, soft cotton rug under your feet on the cabin sole makes a noticeable difference in comfort. A good choice is a washable bath rug with a nonskid ribbed back.
  If you use a rug runner, place cut lengths of rubberized

padding or two-faced tape under the rug to prevent slipping. Treat cut rug ends with white glue to prevent the yarn from unraveling.

HANGING PICTURES   Use brass hinges to hang pictures on the bulkhead; lightweight frames can be hung with Velcro.

SLAT VENETIAN BLINDS   Thin slat venetian blinds are a decorative alternative to curtains on pilot house windows. To prevent them from rattling, hook the lower bar of the blind to the bulkhead.

REFLECTIVE FILM   See-through reflective film, sold in automotive stores, can be attached to ports and hatch covers to lower the cabin temperature on hot days and to give you more privacy.

VENTILATION   Wind passing over an opening causes air to be drawn out of the space below. This phenomenon is called the *Venturi effect*. To draw in air, mount a tent-like cowl over a hatch with the opening facing forward into the wind. Pointing the opening away from the wind will exhaust air from below.

Hatch covers raised on pins will also exhaust hot air from below.

Another way to create the Venturi effect is to install hatch covers that open either forward or backward as needed.

SEACOCKS   Through-the-hull fittings create an extremely vulnerable point in your hull. Inspect them regularly by opening and closing the valves. Make certain that the double stainless steel clamps at the hose connections are tight. Be sure to have a wood plug taped to the hose near the seacock for emergency use.

BILGE ALARM   As an added precaution against flooding below, set up a two-float bilge alarm. The lower float will activate the automatic bilge pump. If water reaches the second float, which has been set a few inches above the first, it will trip the alarm and start a heavy-duty backup pump.

It is probable that you will not hear the bilge alarm from

the cockpit when the engine is running. Install a red flashing light on the cockpit instrument panel to signal when the bilge alarm sounds.

CLEANING THE BILGE It is important to clean the bilge regularly. First, if needed, try to correct any leaking oil problem. Clean the bilge with a commercial degreaser, and follow with a bilge cleaner. If the boat is wood, add borax to the bilge water. Do not pump this water over the side, but draw it off and dispose of it safely. Once the bilge is dry, remove any oily residue with a TSP cleaner and paint with a good marine enamel.

BILGE PUMP STRAINER The end of the bilge pump hose is located in what is probably the darkest, most inaccessible recess of the bilge. Make it easier to clean a clogged bilge pump strainer by tying a string to it and leading it up to a convenient spot. Pull the string to bring the strainer within reach for cleaning.

12-VOLT ACCESSORIES There are a growing number of appliances, such as coffee makers, toasters, frying pans, shavers, video players, oscillating fans, and fluorescent lights, that operate on 12-volt power. Most have heating elements or motors that draw large amounts of electricity. To avoid draining the battery, they should be used when the engine is running.

GALLEY SLAVES NO MORE

Today's modern conveniences and cooking techniques have made it possible to provide well-balanced and tasty meals on board without investing enormous amounts of time and effort. There are hundreds of innovative ideas toward this end. Many of the best of these are in this section.

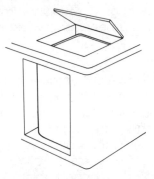

FIGURE 30

HIDDEN TRASH CONTAINER   Get the trash basket off the cabin sole by hiding it away in a galley cabinet. Cut a hole in the countertop and add a ring to the removable piece. It will now open like an ice box. Trash can be deposited through this top "hatch," and the full basket is removed through the cabinet door (see Figure 30).

GALLEY HATCH   Pass food through a hatch cut between the cockpit and the galley. This will allow you to keep the companionway closed during poor weather while the hatch serves as a pass through.

DRAWER STOP   A shallow drawer is easily pulled out too far, spilling its contents on the cabin floor. Tie a restraining string from the back of the drawer to the bulkhead behind. The drawer then cannot pull all the way out.

GALLEY STOOL   If you plan to spend a lot of time in the galley, get a folding stool that can screw into and out of a receptacle in the cabin sole.

FLUORESCENT LIGHT   Flourescent bulbs are seldom used on boats. However, they give excellent light and use little electrical power.

CUTTING BOARD   On the back side of the cutting board, rout out four holes deep enough to hold glasses. You can now use one side for cutting and the other for serving.

Store the cutting board in the wasted space behind the stove.

GALLEY FIDDLES   Replace the countertop edge with 2- to 3-inch-high wood fiddles. These small strips of wood will keep utensils from sliding off the countertop in rough weather.

NONSKID COUNTERTOP   Keep dishes and utensils from sliding around by gluing a nonskid plastic sheet to the counter-top. Rubber mats from bar supply stores will do an equally good job. As a temporary solution, use wet paper towels or even a slice of bread to achieve the same purpose.

NONSKID BOTTOMS   A small bead of silicone sealant put on the bottom of dishes, glasses, and utensils will prevent them from sliding. This works equally well on the bottoms of small appliances, ash trays, navigation tools, and serving trays.

RING HOOKS   Put a cuphook in the bulkhead over the sink. Keep rings, watches, and bracelets on it while doing dishes.

PAPER TOWEL RACK   Hang bulky paper towels and their rack behind the companionway steps, out of the way but easy to reach.

STORAGE IDEAS FOR SMALL OBJECTS   Try using a plastic eyedropper or straws with the ends twisted shut to hold salt, a small screw top jar for sugar, and prescription vials for herbs.

Keep safety matches in an old peanut butter jar. Wrap the outside of the jar with sandpaper, held on with a rubber band, to create a surface on which to scratch the matches.

DISH LOCKER   Stacked dishes can be kept in place in the dish locker by drilling holes in the locker base and inserting pins to hold any size dish snugly (see Figure 31).

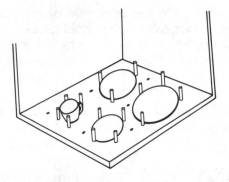

FIGURE 31

VERTICAL PAN STORAGE   Nesting random pots and pans in the locker makes them hard to remove and noisy in rough weather. Partition the locker with four or five vertical plywood sections. Store pots and pans on their side, individually in each section.

VERTICAL DISH STORAGE   Dishes will dry in the dish locker if you store them vertically in a plastic draining rack.

WIRE BINS   Replace original drawers with pull-out wire bins to store dishes. Because of the increased flow of air, the dishes will dry quickly without towel drying.

RACK FOR WINE GLASSES   Wine always tastes better in real glassware—or so it seems. Hang glasses upside down in a locker between parallel, taut shockcords. If you prefer, install a glass rack from a bar supply house.

Most cruisers use unbreakable acrylic glasses that come in every variety, from champagne to water glasses. These are both washable and safe although not as aesthetic as real glass.

GALLEY SINKS   Deep, stainless steel double sinks with drains on opposite sides make the best galley arrangement. Choose the sink on the lee side for good drainage.

CLEANING THE SEAWATER SYSTEM   The seawater sink
hoses will eventually acquire an odor caused by bacteria
growth. Close the through-the-hull connections and allow a
combination of bleach and fresh water to remain in the lines
overnight. After you open the seacock and rinse the lines with
plain water, they should smell fresh again.

As an alternative, try using vinegar or baking soda instead of bleach to clean plastic lines.

CLEANING FIBERGLASS SINK   Use only nonabrasive liquid
cleaners on fiberglass sinks.

POURING HOT LIQUID   Prevent scalding spills by placing
cups in the sink before filling them with hot liquid.

SOAP MAGNET   Keep bar soap out of the way by sticking it
to the sink bulkhead with a magnet. Attach one magnet to
the wall and press a second magnet into the soap.

HALON EXTINGUISHER   Efficient Halon fire extinguishers
do not leave a mess when used in the galley.

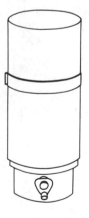

FIGURE 32

THERMOS HOLDER   Attach a Thermos upside down to the
galley bulkhead using a fire extinguisher holder. Use a
threaded plastic spigot in place of the standard screw top

(these are available for Thermoses with No. 4 tops). You now have a safe and convenient way to dispense hot liquids (see Figure 32).

To keep an unmounted Thermos from rolling, bore a hole in the countertop the right size to hold the Thermos snugly.

KEROSENE LAMP   A small, gimbal mounted kerosene lamp provides a pleasing light and does not consume precious electric power.

STOVE PROTECTION   Protect yourself from being thrown against a hot stove by installing an exercise or U-shaped bar in front of the stove.

Or clip a safety harness to a deadeye on the bulkhead to hold yourself in place in rough weather.

Always wear an apron or foul weather trousers to protect yourself from hot spills.

OFFSHORE COOKING   Offshore boats are subject to rough weather during which normal cooking procedures can be hazardous. A good arrangement is to have a small single-burner stove with a fitted pot. They are compact and safe and make a good spare stove, even in calm seas. They can even provide some localized heat if needed.

PROPANE   Propane is becoming increasingly popular and is being used for heating, refrigeration, and cooking. For added safety, connect the propane tank with high-pressure flexible hose rather than with rigid tubing, which has a tendency to loosen.

PROPANE BOTTLES   Because propane gas is heavier than air, avoid keeping propane bottles below deck. Store the bottles securely in deck lockers that are themselves well fastened to the deck. Be sure to put drain holes in the lockers.

Aluminum bottles are easier to maintain than are steel bottles, but they are many times more expensive. Rust prevention and frequent painting will keep steel bottles in perfect shape.

ALCOHOL STOVES   Although they are not as popular to-day as propane gas stoves are, alcohol stoves still have their safety record to recommend them.

To achieve the correct flame setting requires that you adjust the regulator disc. An orange flame means that you should open the regulator disc, and a pulsating flame requires closing the disc slightly.

Put some asbestos rope in the priming cup to keep the alcohol from spilling in rough weather.

LIGHTING THE OVEN   Put a small mirror below the pilot so that you can see the match when you light the oven.

STOVE HEATER   When using the stove as a heater, put a clay pot over a burner on low to better distribute the heat.

THERMAL COOKING   Save cooking fuel by employing thermal cooking techniques. Bring food to a boil, then transfer it to a well-insulated container. Cooking will continue for a time from the retained heat.

ESTIMATING REMAINING FUEL   The only way to determine the amount of fuel remaining in your cooking fuel bottle is by weight. Weigh a full bottle on a 50-pound fisherman's scale. After using, weigh again to estimate how much fuel remains.

NEW WATER TANKS   When you need additional water storage on the boat, consider flexible rubber tanks that fit into various shaped spaces. These tanks should be attached low amidships and secured tightly.

PURIFYING THE WATER SYSTEM   Boiling is not recommended for purifying water. The best approach is to use the recommended dosage of chlorine bleach to remove most germs. Filtering or boiling the water will remove the chlorine odor and make the taste acceptable.

WATER FILTER   Department stores carry activated charcoal taste and odor filters that can make a dramatic improvement in the quality of drinking water on the boat. If you also add halogen tablets and boil the water, the taste will be further improved.

GALLEY SEAWATER   To conserve the freshwater supply, use seawater whenever possible. Seawater can be made available at the galley sink by installing a seawater foot pump. Do the final dish rinsing with small quantities of fresh water.

A bucket is still the least expensive and most maintenance-free solution for getting sea water to the galley sink (or anywhere else it may be needed).

CANNED FOOD INSPECTION   Check canned food, especially if it has been home processed, before using it. If the can's ends pop in and out, don't taste the contents; just discard them.

PRESSURE COOKER   The pressure cooker is essential in the galley. Because it prepares food in far less time than usual, fuel is saved and less heat is generated in the galley. All nutrients and taste are retained. Nothing is more versatile than the pressure cooker, which can bake, boil, braise, and steam.

ROUGH WEATHER MEALS   Soups, stews, and other foods prepackaged in boilable plastic bags are easy to prepare when you must cook in rough weather. Pop them into a pressure cooker for a hot meal in minutes.

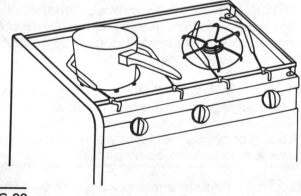

FIGURE 33

POT HOLDERS Stainless steel rods, which are sold at marine supply stores, can be attached to the stove fiddle to hold a pot securely over its burner (see Figure 33).

DOUBLE BOILER A drip coffee pot can perform extra duty if it is also used as a double boiler.

WOK On calm days, try using a wok. It will cook food quickly and sit securely on its frame over the burner.

NESTING COOKWARE Nesting stainless steel cook sets that include a frying pan, two sauce pans, and a utility pot take up less than a cubic foot of space. Most have removable handles so that when they are stored nested, they are a great space saver.

SAVE BURNED PAN Don't throw a pot over the side because it's marred with burned-on food. Simply put an inch of water with a small amount of detergent in the pot and boil on the stove for a few minutes. The cooked-on food will wash right off.

LONG-TERM FOOD STORAGE Dehydrated foods sealed in cans in a nitrogen atmosphere will last for many years. Regular cans should be coated with WD-40 and sealed in plastic bags to increase their shelf life.

Fresh eggs can be identified if they sink in salt water (spoiled eggs will float). After selecting fresh eggs, put them in a jar completely filled with a brine solution. They will keep for six months or more. For shorter storage periods, coat the eggs with Vaseline or wax, and turn them weekly.

Garlic buds will keep almost indefinitely if they are kept in a closed jar with enough cooking oil to cover them.

Olive oil will also keep indefinitely if it is kept tightly sealed.

CHEESE STORAGE Cheese will keep longer if wrapped in moistened cheese cloth or waxed on the cut surface. Keep in a cool place.

Prevent cheese mold from growing by enclosing cheese in a container with some sugar.

DARK STORAGE   Onions, potatoes, apples, oranges, carrots, and cabbage will keep longer if wrapped lightly, so they do not touch each other, and kept in a cool, dark place. Unripened vegetables and fruits that have been wiped with bleach and wrapped in paper store quite well.

Pop any sprouting shoots off potatoes, and they will keep longer.

JUICE STORAGE   Two aspirin tablets dissolved in a quart of lemon or lime juice will preserve the juice for up to a month.

To extract a small amount of juice without wasting the fruit, prick a small hole in any citrus fruit and squeeze out just the needed quantity.

Use lemon or lime gelatin as a substitute when you need citrus flavor but have no fresh fruit.

AIR-TIGHT PACKAGING   To remove air from a food storage bag and achieve a vacuum seal, immerse a half-filled Ziploc bag in water up to the opening and seal it. Fold over the empty half and place the bag into a second Ziploc bag. Seal the second bag following the same procedure.

FOOD PACKAGING   Purchase perishable foods in packaging that will maintain its integrity in a damp icebox environment.

VACUUM PACKAGING   Fresh meat and bread will keep longer if you vacuum seal them at home before taking them on your sailing trip.

CANNED FOODS   Canned meat, butter, and cheese travel well on long trips. Consider using canned hearts of palm or asparagus spears in place of a salad. Canned potatoes are quite good when sliced and fried.

DRIED FRUIT   To preserve fresh fruit for an extended period, add water, simmer small slices of fruit for 10 minutes. Dry the slices with paper toweling, then heat them in the oven for 10 more minutes at 200 degrees F. Seal them in plastic bags, squeezing out as much air as possible.

JAPANESE DRIED SOUP   Wonderful dehydrated soups from Japan, called ramen, are easy to prepare and delicious, especially on a cold day.

DRIED SALAMI   It is amazing how long salamis and other hard sausages will last without refrigeration if they are left in their casings.

PICKLING   Long-voyage cruisers take along extra vinegar and salt so that they can pickle and salt food during the trip.

YOGURT   For long-distance cruisers, yogurt can be made from powdered milk, canned milk, and freeze-dried yogurt starter.

BACON   Rub a bacon slab with vinegar, and wrap it in cheese cloth for long storage. If mold forms, it can usually be cut or scraped off.

HANDLING WINE   Some California wines are available in boxed plastic bags. This might be the answer to the storage and disposal of bulky wine bottles.

Cool bottles of wine by hanging them over the side in mesh bags.

If you lose the cork, put a candle stub in the top to seal an unfinished bottle of wine.

Use a wine bottle as a rolling pin.

SUN TEA   Tea brewed in a glass jar that is rocking gently in the sun can make the best iced tea you have ever had.

FOOD FOR A QUEASY STOMACH   Some basic, easy-to-digest foods for the first few days at sea are split pea soup, hard boiled eggs, and plain crackers. Bouillon cube soup provides good, quick nourishment and is easy to prepare at sea. In fact, soup is perfect to start the day on a cold morning.

TOAST   Grill bread in a frying pan to make toast.

POPCORN　Unpopped popcorn keeps very well and always provides an easily prepared treat on the boat.

SPROUTS　Almost any seed will successfully grow sprouts. Place seeds in an open-mouth glass jar without soil. Lean the jar on its side and cover the top with muslin. Rinse the seeds each day and drain off any remaining water.

PEANUT BUTTER　High in protein, peanut butter requires no refrigeration and keeps for a long time.

NUTS　Add nuts and seeds to sandwiches, desserts, and cereals to put extra fiber in your diet and to dress up meals at sea.

FISH　You can always tell if fish are fresh if they float in cold water, have clear eyes, and, of course, smell fresh.

　　　　After handling fish, you can remove the odor from your hands by rinsing them with vinegar or lemon juice.

　　　　Use bleach to cleanse the board you use to prepare the fish.

MUSSELS　Mussels are available in most parts of the world. As with all shellfish, be sure the local waters are uncontaminated before you harvest the mussels. First scrub them, then soak them in cornmeal and water for thorough cleaning. Steam them as you would clams.

CONCH　Eat conch raw, steamed, lime-cured, or as fritters. After cutting the meat from the shell, cut away obvious inedible parts. Tenderize the meat by pounding it flat to twice its original size.

SHELLFISH　Collect shellfish from uncontaminated waters that are open to the sea. The best locations are downwind, near plentiful plankton sources, and in swift-running water. Wear gloves and sneakers, and dig quickly with a rake.

SEAWATER BREAD　Using usual recipes, mix boiled seawater (instead of fresh), sugar, yeast, and flour. To avoid mess, knead the dough in a plastic bag. Remove dough from plastic wrapping and let it rise in a warm place. After it rises, put the dough in a pressure cooker and remove the regulator. When the dough has fully risen, bake for 30 minutes on each side. Put the bread on a cooling rack while it is still hot. The rack will make perfect wire marks on the loaf to show where to slice.

ICEBOX EFFICIENCY   Install vinyl-covered wire shelves for better icebox organization.

Place perishable foods directly on the ice in Ziploc or mesh bags.

FOAM INSULATION   Commercial refrigeration contractors can supply you with pieces of foam to improve the insulation of your icebox.

ICEBOX PUMP   Use a foot-operated pump and hose to remove ice water from the icebox and pump it to a cooler in the cockpit. This super-cold water will chill drinks in the cooler.

CONSERVE ICE   Temporarily plug the drain in the icebox to keep the cold water in the chest. This will help to retain the cold and slow the melting of block ice. Once a day remove the plug to eliminate excess water.

Make crushed ice by hammering chunks of ice in a plastic bag.

Keep ice in a wide-mouth thermos bottle. It will last quite a long time.

FRESH ICEBOX   Keep the icebox smelling fresh by putting in ground coffee, vanilla beans, or baking soda.

ICE TONGS   Why do we use burlap or log carriers to haul ice on board when ice tongs have been doing the best job for ages?

ICEBOX LOADING   Put drinks that are already cold into the icebox to optimize the limited amount of ice. Frozen milk and other foods can actually help lower the overall box temperature.

ICE SELECTION   Dry ice, if it does not touch your food, will supplement regular ice and measurably drop the box temperature.

The best blocks of regular ice are those that are so cold that your fingers stick to them.

BUG PREVENTION   To keep bugs from taking up residence in your dry foods, add a few bay leaves to containers of flour and grains.

THE WELL-CLOTHED SAILOR

An entire section of this chapter is devoted to clothing. We all have a tendency to carry too many or the wrong kind of clothes on board. This section provides ideas on how to better select, pack, store, launder, repair, and even use the clothes that you will bring along.

Be sure to try the following clothes cleaning remedies on a hidden part of the fabric before proceeding.

FIGURE 34

ON-BOARD WASHING MACHINE   Put dirty laundry, water, and detergent in a closed bucket in a lazaret. A few hours of swishing about will clean the clothes.

Alternatively, you can clean clothes in a bucket by using a toilet plunger to provide a washing machine kind of agitation (see Figure 34).

TOW DIRTY CLOTHES Tie a few items of clothing to a long line, and tow them for an hour behind the boat. Rinse in fresh water and dry.

DRIED BLOOD IN CLOTHING After you have rinsed the blood-stained garment at length in cold water, soak it in ammonia and cold water or in enzyme presoak and warm water. As noted earlier, all chemicals used on clothing should be tested for color fastness.

REMOVING MILDEW FROM LEATHER Wipe mildew off with a diluted solution of rubbing alcohol and apply leather polish.

MILDEW IN CLOTHING Wash mildewed clothes in detergent. Then apply lemon juice and salt to the mildewed areas and leave to bleach in the sun.

ASPHALT IN CLOTHING Don't set the stain with water. Scrape off the excess asphalt, soften the remaining stain with Vaseline, and sponge with turpentine. Then, when the stain is gone, clean the article with soap and water.

PACKING A SEABAG Sailors in navies throughout the world have perfected a way of packing clothes that few of us use. Get a large seabag with a full side zipper. Waterproof PVC-coated Dacron bags are available. Roll clothes loosely and pack, putting shoes in the end, breakable items in the center, and the toilet kit on top. Fill in all the gaps with loose items.

CLOTHES STORAGE The musty smell that clothes get in drawers on the boat can be prevented by putting open bars of scented soap, activated charcoal, baking soda, or sheets of fabric softener in with the clothes.

Most of the clothing you bring on board can be stored in

pillow cases and stuck in hideaway corners to save valuable drawer and locker space.

Keep the rare pair of pantyhose safe from snagging by storing it in a resealable plastic bag.

SCENTED SHOE BAGS
Sneakers, deck shoes, and boots develop an odor when they remain damp. Sew cedar chips into 8-inch-long tubes of loose cotton cloth. Insert these tubes into the shoes to give them and the locker a fresh scent. Dust baking soda into the shoe to help kill any remaining offensive odors.

CARE OF WET BOAT SHOES
If your deck shoes get soaked with salt water, rinse them with fresh water. Air-dry them away from heat after stuffing them with paper towels. Use saddle soap or neat's-foot oil to soften the leather, then wax them with shoe polish. If you tie leather laces tight when they are wet, they will not easily come loose.

To remove salt from shoes, soak them in vinegar and fresh water and dry them in the sun.

Or try rubbing the leather with a raw potato, allowing the starch to draw out the salt. Rinse, dry thoroughly, and polish.

FIGURE 35

FOUL WEATHER BOOTS
Buy your boots one size larger than your shore shoes so that they can be worn comfortably with heavy socks.

To prevent water from entering your boots, slip a 2-inch

piece of inner tube over your foul weather pants and extend it down and to just over the boot top.

When you get out of your foul weather pants and boots, push the trousers down over the boot top and step out. They will now be much easier to get into when you next need them (see Figure 35).

Put a couple of empty paper towel tubes or rolled-up magazines in boots to stand them upright.

TIGHT SHOES Dried-out deck shoes are stiff and tight. Rub any tight spot with alcohol, and put the shoes on while the spots are still wet to help reset the original shape. Polish to protect the leather.

STUCK ZIPPERS WD-40 sprayed on a poorly running zipper will often make it work like new.

HANGERS Keep clothes from sliding off hangers by putting several rubber bands on the hanger shoulders. Clothespins are also useful in fastening garments to wire hangers.

OLD IRON Remove the cord from an old iron and keep the iron on board. When a quick pressing is in order, heat up the iron on the stove.

COLD WEATHER PROTECTION Research continues to prove the advantages of layering clothes to keep warm and dry. First put on a polypropylene or silk undergarment. Next, add a second layer of pants and shirts. Synthetic fabrics dry more quickly. However, if wool is used, put synthetic layers over and under it. The final layer is the waterproof foul weather gear. Velcro fasteners at the neck and cuffs provide a snug seal. Wearing a terry cloth towel around your neck helps prevent water from leaking down your back. Socks made from a blend of wool, polypropylene, and nylon are fast drying and warm in wet boots.

LOST GLASSES If your reading glasses went over the side and the chart is indecipherable, poke a small hole in a piece of paper and look at the chart through the hole. It is amazing how clear a small part of the chart becomes. This clever trick will not be necessary if you keep an extra pair of glasses on board.

READING GLASSES
Bifocals that have the top lens made from high-quality tinted glass and the lower lens made from magnifying glass are a good choice for those sailors who need reading glasses only. These are available in the better sporting goods catalogs.

In the same catalogs there are quick-flip magnifiers that clip to most sunglasses. They can flip up out of the way when you are through reading a chart.

MOUNTAINEERS' GLASSES
There are available excellent sunglasses with headbands, commonly used by mountaineers, that slip over prescription glasses. They include a detachable nose protector to prevent sunburn. They do an equally good job for sailors who have the same hot sun and reflected glare to control.

MONOCULARS
Monoculars are often preferred by people who have difficulty adjusting to binoculars. They can usually be found in the more exotic sporting goods stores.

BINOCULARS
Binoculars with 7×50 magnification have long been the sailor's favorite for good reason. They produce a wide, steady magnification ideally suited to the sailor's need. Recently popular are binoculars with shock-absorbing armor and a built-in compass. If you wear eyeglasses, it is best to select a pair of binoculars with the highest field of view. This allows your eyes, behind glasses, to be farther away from the lens and still get a clear view.

KEEPING GREENWICH TIME
Keep a separate digital watch on board that is set to Greenwich time. This will help to avoid any confusion over time changes when you perform navigation calculations.

THE HEAD: THE NECESSARY NECESSARY

Maintenance and repair of the head are covered extensively in manufacturer's manuals and marine publications. Some additional ideas on easy ways to make the head more efficient, sanitary, and comfortable ought to be welcome on any boat.

A NO-SPILL HEAD   If the head fills up with water when the boat heels over, replace the intake hose with a longer version. Arch the hose above the water line and add a vented loop.

FLEXIBLE HOSE   Replace the present head piping with flexible reinforced hose. Should there be a stoppage, bending and squeezing the hose will often clear it.

LUBRICATE THE HEAD   You will be surprised to find that a small amount of cooking or hydraulic oil added to the head water will make pumping easier. Do not use lubrication oil.

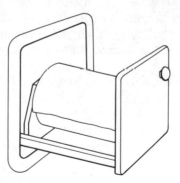

FIGURE 36

TOILET TISSUE   Clogging the head mechanism is less likely if specially formulated marine toilet tissue is used.

By cutting a hole in the bulkhead, you can make an arrangement to allow the toilet roll and bar to slide in and out, drawer fashion, saving much needed space (see Figure 36).

BATH TOWELS   Use quick drying small towels or cloth diapers rather than large terry cloth towels, which take days to dry.

LIQUID SOAP   Cut a hole in the head counter top to hold a liquid soap container that has a pump. Or mount the container on the bulkhead with Velcro. You can make liquid soap at home in a blender using small pieces of leftover bath soap.

BAR SOAP   If you must use bar soap, avoid the usual mess by keeping it in the foil wrapper or resting it on a sponge.

To get longer use from small slivers of soap, place a number of these in a mesh bag hung by the sink.

STOWING THE GEAR

Let's work toward more accessible storage in the cabin area. Space is often lost in blind corners, in the galley, and under bunks. After living with the boat for a while, you will determine your particular needs. You can then decide whether structural changes or better organization will best serve your purpose. Every small idea that prevents clutter and loose items lying about will improve living conditions below.

STORAGE CYLINDERS   Short lengths of PVC pipe with end caps screwed on the bottom, attached to the bulkhead with Velcro, are great containers for a variety of items. They can be sealed for moisture protection with another end cap on the top. Plastic welding rod cylinders are also excellent for similar storage.

HEAT-SEALED BAGS   A great variety of foods, spare parts, and electronic pieces can be stored in heat-sealed plastic bags. Humidity problems can be prevented by including a silica gel packet in each bag. Calculators, stop watches, and cameras can be operated while still safely sealed in a plastic bag.

SHOE BAG STORAGE   Buy a compartmented canvas organizer with six to ten shoebox-sized pockets. Shirts, sweaters, shoes, towels, sheets, glasses, charts, and many other items can be stored in this organizer. Hang the bag on the back of a locker door where it will have good ventilation and be easy to reach. Put a small cedar board or herb potpourri in the bottom of each pocket.

For a smaller version of this arrangement, hang a carpenter's apron on another locker door to hold heavy items such as power tools, large wrenches, and hammers.

Hang another apron of this type in the galley to store bulky garbage bags, paper towels, plastic wrap, and detergent bottles.

BLANKET STORAGE   Fold bulky blankets and sheets flat, and store them under bunk mattresses.

CAN STORAGE   Stack up to four cans and tape them together into long cylinders. Store them in the dead space behind berths. Wrap cloth around the cans to keep them from rattling.

COLLAPSIBLE MILK CRATES   Plastic milk crates are good for storing and carrying just about anything, but they take up too much space on the boat. You can now buy collapsible milk crates that fold to a 3-inch height.

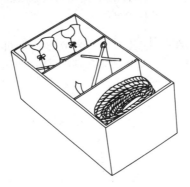

FIGURE 37

LAZARET STORAGE   To have a better organized cockpit lazaret, divide it into three compartments using plywood partitions. Place life jackets in one compartment. You can store coiled lines and the spare anchor separately in other compartments (see Figure 37).

BILGE STORAGE   Remove paper labels from cans and identify the contents on the lid with indelible ink. Seal cans in plastic bags and store them in the bilge.

WATERTIGHT STORAGE   There are many kinds of waterproof containers to keep cameras, tools, lenses, charts, flares, batteries, electrical parts, binoculars, or any other water-sensitive items safe. Army/Navy stores carry ammunition boxes and water storage sacks. Fishing supply stores often have large plastic boxes with gasketed lids. It takes little time or money to fashion a good case from 4-inch diameter PVC pipe with screw-on end caps. Make the container shock proof by padding the bottoms or filling the voids with foam. Label the outside with the name of the equipment that is sealed in the container. Silica gel packets from a camera store will absorb any moisture in the containers.

SMALL STORAGE CONTAINERS   Empty 35-millimeter film containers are great for storing small items. Label the outside and fill with shampoo, first aid lotion, matches, or small electrical parts.

   A small box in a locker will help to collect those tiny items that you find all over the boat.

COMPANIONWAY SLIDES   Get those bulky companionway slides off the aft bunk, and attach them securely to the bulkhead with shockcord.

CHAPTER 4

SAFETY

Everyone shares a common concern for safety. In spite of this, most of us are generally quite lax in making our homes, our cars, and our workplace free of hazards. The boat is usually an exception in this regard. Sailors, by necessity, are careful people who try to use anticipation and prevention as their ultimate safety measures.

KEEPING HEALTHY

On a short trip, concerns about staying healthy are probably limited to seasickness, personal comfort, and hygiene. On a longer voyage, this concern can be expanded to include emergency care of injuries and sickness when medical help is not easily accessible. Medical advice is probably best obtained by radio contact. However, levelheaded short-term care can stabilize and often measurably relieve a medical problem. Sailors are often isolated and therefore must be prepared to cope with any unexpected situation.

FACTS ABOUT HYPOTHERMIA Most of the earth's ocean waters are below 70 degrees Fahrenheit. This will cause the human body, with its temperature of 98.6 degrees, to rapidly lose heat in the ocean. Heat loss occurs 30 to 35 times faster in water than in air of the same temperature. When your body temperature drops to 94 degrees Fahrenheit, you lose control of your limbs. At 86 degrees Fahrenheit, you will begin to lose consciousness.

FIGURE 38

PREVENTION OF HYPOTHERMIA　　If an emergency occurs and you become aware that you will be in the water for a long time, use the following precautions to prevent excessive heat loss. Relax and consider your options. Keep your clothes on; they will help to preserve heat next to the body. Tight clothes hold heat better; loose clothing allows water to wash over your body. You can breathe warm air down into a buttoned up foul weather jacket (see Figure 38).

The greatest heat loss occurs from your neck and head so keep them above the water if possible. In fact, you will retain body heat longer if you can get most of your body out of the water and onto anything floating. Keep as still as possible. If more than one person is in the water, body heat loss can be reduced if you huddle together.

The best way to conserve strength and body heat in the water is to float in a relaxed fetal position. Raise your head to breathe and return to the crouched floating position. It is, in fact, easier to float in this position than on your back.

RECOVERY FROM HYPOTHERMIA　　If medical help is not available and you must treat a hypothermia victim, it is advisable to warm the patient's skin surface slowly. Warm the central portion of the body by putting warm, wet towels on the stomach. Work slowly out toward the limbs.

PREVENTION OF SEASICKNESS   Sensory conflict is the proper name for seasickness. Once you realize why it occurs, postponement and prevention are possible. When you first experience some queasiness, get busy, stay on deck in the center of the boat, and keep the horizon in view. Going to sleep is a good idea if you can.

FIGURE 39

CURES FOR SEASICKNESS   If seasickness still occurs after following the foregoing preventive measures, try some of the following ideas.

Continue to eat regularly, but eat easily digestible foods such as broth and crackers.

To be effective, prescription drugs and skin patches for seasickness must be used before symptoms occur.

Some sailors find that listening to music through headsets helps take their mind off the nausea. The music may cause some disruption of the sensory conflict.

Pressing on the accupressure point located above your wrist on the inside, about three fingers up from the wrist crease and between the two tendons, will give temporary relief (see Figure 39). Accupressure wrist bands are sold in marine stores.

NASA is training astronauts to use biofeedback to deal with motion sickness.

EAR PATCHES Wash your hands after placing anti-seasickness patches behind your ears. Rubbing your eyes with the medication on your hands can produce considerable discomfort.

AIR SICKNESS BAGS The next time you take an airplane trip, collect a few of the air sickness bags. Kept on the boat, they might make a bout of seasickness more dignified for an embarrassed guest.

SPLINTERS First numb the splinter area with a piece of ice. Find the exact location of the splinter by staining it with iodine. Sterilize a needle and remove the splinter carefully. Now treat it as you would a puncture wound.

CUTS AND BRUISES Keep one or two chemically activated cold packs, like the ones used by sports teams, on the boat. They produce intense cold for about 15 minutes and help to reduce swelling from a bruise. A chunk of ice in a cloth also does a good job.

When medicating a cut or abrasion, apply antiseptic ointment to the bandage, not to the wound.

TOOTHPASTE SUBSTITUTES Natural tooth cleaners will suffice if you run out of the drugstore variety. Neutralize mouth acids and freshen your breath by brushing with salt or baking soda or by chewing sugar-free gum. Use dental floss regularly.

SALTWATER BATHING You can give yourself a seawater shower on deck using a garden spray tank. Just a few pumps produce a fine strong spray and use little water. Always choose a spray tank that has been used only for carrying water.

Most dish detergents or hair shampoos will lather in salt water.

Use fabric softener or vinegar as a freshwater hair rinse and conditioner.

NATURAL HOT WATER Make your own hot-water deck shower. Attach a hose and triggered nozzle to a 3-cubic-foot, black, heavy, plastic bag. Fill the bag with water and raise it 6 feet with a halyard. The black plastic will absorb heat and provide hot water for a shower.

SHAMPOO SUBSTITUTES A small amount of cornstarch or baby powder rubbed into your hair and brushed out absorbs excess oils and acts as a dry shampoo.

COOL OFF A rapid way to cool your body temperature on a scorching day is to run cold water over your wrists. The water cools the blood vessels near the skin surface and gives you an almost instant feeling of relief.

SUNBURN Vitamin E oil, applied to the skin directly from the vitamin capsule, has relieved many painful sunburns. Often the burn will disappear overnight. Other rich sources of Vitamin E are common cooking oils from safflower, sunflower and cotton seed. Vitamin A and D ointment, available in any drugstore, is also excellent for burns of any kind.

INSECT BITES Cornstarch, vinegar, and baking soda help soothe insect bites. Ammonia will take the itch out of mosquito bites. It is also advisable to keep an emergency bee sting kit on board.

SHAVING Before shaving, soften whiskers with mineral oil.
Wet and dry battery-operated shavers do an excellent job, either dry or with shaving cream or mineral oil.

SECURITY

A few ideas follow to help you cope with the escalating problem of boat security. Although the prevention of vandalism and thievery cannot be totally guaranteed, making the boat a less attractive, more difficult target will often discourage the amateur intruder.

CONTENTS OF BOAT VIDEO TAPE
Video tape or photograph all locker and lazaret contents. Lay out and photograph all electronic, navigational, and personal equipment. Should there be a theft, the film, kept at home, will be evidence of ownership.

Cut a credit card in half and drop it behind some hidden place on the boat. Then, if there is ever a question of the boat's ownership, having the card there can prove ownership pretty conclusively.

FIGURE 40

SAFETY HARNESS SECURITY
At sea, always wear a safety harness at night or whenever weather conditions warrant shortening the sail.

There is always a possibility that the safety harness spring clip attached to a deck U-bolt will open by itself if it is twisted 180 degrees (see Figure 40). It is important to be aware of this phenomenon and use extra care.

To make getting into the harness easier, wear a flotation jacket with a sewn-on safety harness.

Harnesses used by parachutists and mountaineers may also provide certain advantages to the sailor. These harnesses have quick disconnect mechanisms, locking carabiners, a figure-eight configuration, and very heavy webbing.

Rig the safety harness line from bow to stern with just

enough slack so that it will pull taut a few feet above the surface of the water should you go overboard. If it is taut, you can get a good hold for pulling yourself back on board.

BURGLAR ALARM   Boat burglar alarms are available that activate when the boat's natural displacement is changed by someone getting on board or towing the boat. Normal wave motion does not affect it.

PROTECTION AGAINST THEFT   Mark the inflatable with your boat's name and number, and there will be less chance of losing it to thieves. Paint your boat's name and number on the side of the bow, and burn the same information into the oars and outboard engine cowling.

THEFTPROOF OUTBOARD   Lead a ¾-inch plastic-covered motorcycle cable through the outboard motor mount and around a stern stanchion. Hold it fast with a large padlock.

FIGURE 41

SINGLEHANDED SECURITY   Most singlehanded bluewater sailors trail a long line from the stern as a safety precaution. To improve on this idea, attach this line to the tiller, then to a stanchion with light twine, then over the stern. A singlehander in the water needs only to grab the trailing line to jam the tiller over (see Figure 41). This will put the boat quietly into the wind.

You can provide added security by trailing an additional short line from the stern swim ladder. A tug on this line will drop the ladder, making it easier for a tired person to reboard the boat.

FUEL LEAK DETECTOR   You can lower most insurance policy rates by installing a fuel leak detector and an automatic fire extinguisher system.

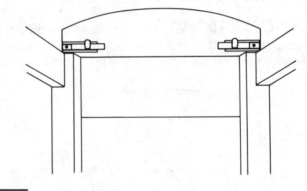

FIGURE 42

COMPANIONWAY SLIDE LOCKS   To improve cabin security, bolt companionway boards from inside. Attach deadbolts on either side of the companionway and drill holes in the sides of the companionway boards. When the bolts are thrown, you will feel more secure below (see Figure 42).

RADAR REFLECTORS   Place wrinkled aluminum foil inside an aluminum or wooden mast to improve your radar visibility. A radar-reflecting flag of anodized silver is claimed to be radar visible for up to eight miles.

WINDOW SECURITY If you are concerned about port hole or pilot house window security, replace the glass with impact resistant, clear acrylic. Tinted acrylic will add to your privacy.

TAMPER-RESISTANT HINGES To secure a hinge with outside hinge pins, remove one screw from each hinge leaf and drive a double-headed rust-proof nail into the jam.

DISABLE A DIESEL To prevent your diesel from being started by an unauthorized person, you can temporarily disable the engine. Remove the air filter cover and strainer, and put a small wooden plug into the air intake pipe. Replace the cover and strainer. This will block the air supply and prevent the engine from starting.

STORM SECURITY Prepare for a strong blow by having on board storm shutters for all port holes.

WHAT IF—?

Every precaution can be taken, and still emergencies arise. When emergencies do occur, keep a cool head and try to contain the problem so that it does not escalate.

Except in most acute situations, the boat is usually moving slowly enough to give you time to assess the problem and implement the correct response. Fire and man overboard are two emergencies in which this is not true. In these events, every crewmember should know what to do immediately and instinctively—delay does nothing but increase the danger. Don't get into the mind set of "this can't happen to me." Expect to encounter all problems someday, and be prepared by conducting safety drills and rehearsing "what if" solutions in advance.

DAMAGE CONTROL Include a section in the ship's notebook on how to deal with a major collision. This information will identify all seacock locations and show where emergency repair equipment is stored. The repair equipment should be kept in a labeled canvas bag. Include a hacksaw, underwater epoxy putty, wedges, wood plugs, pieces of wood, hose clamps, packing cloth, and an axe.

LIFE RAFT SURVIVAL KIT   Much has been written about the necessary contents of a life raft survival kit. Items often omitted from these lists include a parafoil kite to elevate the radio antenna and to tow the raft in a decent wind. An Emergency Position Indicating Radio Beacon (EPIRB) is an absolute essential in today's world of advanced electronics. Also include sun block cream or lotion and a fish gaff to bring a large fish into the raft.

LIFE RAFT   In a severe storm, keep the emergency raft inflated and tied down, ready to go at a moment's notice.

EMERGENCY PILOTING   How can you navigate into a harbor if you are a few miles offshore and don't have a chart? On a piece of graph paper, mark the latitude and longitude of known lights and buoys. You can find this information in the published light list. From these data, you can plot headings to your destination.

ELECTRICAL FAILURE   If you have a complete electrical failure at sea but need to start the engine, remove all connections to the battery except those leading from the battery to the starter. Run a wire from the battery positive terminal to the coil primary switch side. Start the engine by grounding the small solenoid terminal on the starter with a screwdriver. Stop the engine by uncoupling the coil wire.

CABIN FLOODING   A flooded cabin can be cleared of water only after the leak has been discovered and stopped. Check for a broken engine cooling line if the problem occurred while the engine was running. If a lot of water shows up in the bilge, the engine may be pumping water into the boat.

After the leak has been repaired, try to expel large amounts of water with a manual diaphragm pump. To avoid admitting more water in rough weather, leave the smallest possible opening in the companionway hatch, large enough only to accommodate the discharge end of the pump hose.

Remember, dumping buckets full of water into the galley sink is the simplest way to remove water quickly.

To use the head as a bilge pump, first close the seacock and disconnect the hose. Place the end of the intake hose into the bilge and remove water by pumping the head.

To prevent taking on water by the through-the-hull fittings when heeling hard over, lengthen the hoses and loop them up to deck level. As an alternative, install check valves in the through-the-hull hoses. The valves will close when water runs in the reverse direction.

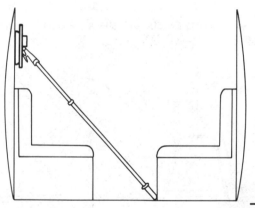

FIGURE 43

TEMPORARY HOLING REPAIR   Place a cushion against the hole from the inside. Cover it with a flat piece of wood and hold it tight against the bulkhead by jamming it into place with a boathook (see Figure 43).

To repair a small hole, soak a rag in epoxy putty and jam it tightly into the hole. If you don't have epoxy putty, stuff a rag into the hole and hammer a peg or stick into the rag, sealing the hole.

SLOW BILGE LEAK   Find a bilge leak through a process of elimination. First check the through-the-hulls. If they are sound, check for leaks in the hull. Plug a midship limber hole to determine which side of the hull is leaking water. Keep plugging limber holes until you find the exact location of the leak.

MAN OVERBOARD

A well-trained crew is prepared for the maneuvers necessary when a man is over the side, which should never be treated as anything but an emergency.

First, get the man-overboard pole, Lifesling, and cushions into the water. Set the dinghy loose if conditions permit.

Toss the Lifesling toward the victim. Sail around the person in the water in circles of decreasing diameter until the line makes contact with him. Once he has the U-shaped sling under his arms, he can be pulled to the boat and winched aboard using the tackle on the Lifesling.

WHISTLE

Attach a plastic whistle to each life ring and personal flotation device (PFD).

FIGURE 44

MAN OVERBOARD RECOVERY

Prepare in advance a boathook with a securely attached loop on one end and a lifting eye on the other. Lean over the side, and get the person in the water to put the loop under his arms. Then winch him aboard after attaching the halyard to the lifting eye on the end of the pole (see Figure 44).

It is very difficult to haul a person back on board using a halyard alone. Therefore, to increase the effectiveness of the procedure, you must create additional leverage. Rig a three- to four-part tackle between the person in the water and an extra winch. By hauling on both lines, you will make the task much easier.

Dropping the mainsail into the water as a sling is another way to bring a casualty back on the boat.

All the foregoing rescue measures are very difficult and require well-trained teamwork to succeed. Conduct frequent man overboard drills to perfect your techniques.

FIRE Quick response will save the day if a fire breaks out on the boat. One crewmember should turn the boat downwind to keep the fire out of the cockpit. Put one of the crew in the dinghy, positioned to rescue the others if the fire gets out of control.

You may need to use great quantities of water if the fire extinguishers can't cope with the fire. Plan for this contingency in advance by having buckets in accessible storage.

Fiberglass roving, often kept on hand for repairs, can be used to smother a fire.

Alcohol fires can be put out with water, grease fires with baking soda, and electronic fires with Halon extinguishers. Use Halon because it does not make a mess and ruin electronic equipment.

There are two distinct advantages to using a heat-acti- vated fire extinguisher in the engine room. First, it may well start up before you even know that there is a fire. Second, because the extinguisher decreases the need for you to open the engine room door, the fire will be starved of needed oxygen.

LIGHTNING If you are caught unprepared in a lightning storm, drop a length of chain from a chainplate into the water as a temporary ground.

If possible, drop anchor, go below and keep everyone away from metal objects.

EMERGENCY STEERING   The next time the boat is out of the water, drill a small hole in the top of the trailing edge of the rudder and put a plug in the hole. If you should ever lose your steering, pop out the plug and pass a line through the hole to allow you to pull the rudder in either direction.

If you have lost the rudder, use the sails to steer the boat.

You can also drag a line over the stern on either side to change the boat's direction.

FOULED PROP   A first approach to clearing a fouled prop is to have one person turn the engine flywheel in the reverse direction while another person pulls on the line that has fouled the prop. This may be adequate to unwind the line and preclude your having to go into the water.

If you must go in the water, it will be easier to saw the line rather than cut it. Use a serrated knife or a hacksaw.

EMERGENCY SIGNALS   If you are trying to get another vessel's attention in an emergency, use a mirror to flash a signal to the other boat. Whether you flash in code or not, it will attract their interest.

Other ways to send a signal are to use a dye marker, strobe light, flare, flashlight, horn, or even to wave your arms.

GOING AGROUND   When first aground, check the depth around the boat to find the way to deeper water, which will often be in the direction of your approach. Kedge off by carrying the anchor out in the dinghy or by swimming it out on a life vest. Drop the anchor as far out as possible in the direction you wish to go. Lead the anchor line through a chock to a large winch and use the winch to pull the boat back into deep water. Shift weight to the bow by directing the crew forward. This will raise the stern, where the boat is probably caught. To avoid damaging the rudder, be sure it is centered before you begin to back off.

EMERGENCY WATER STILLS Research has shown that an adult requires up to two quarts of water per day to sustain good health. There are solar water stills that can convert salt water to fresh water in this quantity. These stills are composed of two-part bags that float in the water. Salt water placed in one bag wicks through a permeable membrane to deposit fresh water in the adjoining section.

BROKEN MAST A broken mast floating in the water beside the boat presents a grave danger. To protect the boat from being holed, tie a mattress between the mast and the boat's topside. Next, remove the cotter pins from the shrouds and bring as much of the mast and rigging on board as possible. Rapid removal of the standing rigging is possible if you have used brass cotter pins in the lower clevis pin of every shroud and stay. You should not have to use any tools; the brass cotter pins can be removed by hand.

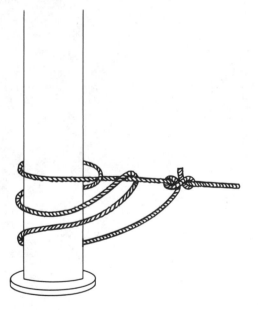

FIGURE 45

TOWING KNOT If you are being towed, use a knot that can be quickly untied. Pass the towing line around the mast, over the standing part of the line and around the mast in the opposite direction, over the standing part of the line again and around the mast in the original direction. Tie it off with a few hitches (see Figure 45).

FLOTATION JACKETS   Consider buying flotation vests or jackets for your crew. The real advantage of these devices is that you are more likely to wear them than traditional life preservers because they are good looking, comfortable, and not bulky.

CHAPTER 5

~~~

BOAT HANDLING

In previous parts of the book, we have dealt with the boat itself and how to improve it. Now we will explore some sailing techniques, including better anchoring and docking procedures, handling the boat in stormy weather, and navigation.

The last section is devoted to weather. Although this is a complex subject, mastering some basic facts can give any sailor a good weather sense.

ANCHORING: THE PROPER HOOK

Sailors must feel certain that everything possible has been done to secure their boat before they leave to go ashore or when they go to sleep at night. Much has been written about anchoring. This section is a collection of the most helpful of these hints. There are tips on anchoring as a singlehander, ideas for recovering a fouled anchor, and techniques to make the boat ride more comfortably in a swell or high wind.

PREPARATION FOR ANCHORING   When anchoring in a swift current, flake the anchor line on the deck to an estimated length and cleat it down. If the rode runs out rapidly, it will not get away from you.

PICKING UP MOORING To prepare for picking up a mooring, allow the sails to luff. Estimate the amount of carry to bring the boat to a full stop. Then round up into the wind from the correct distance, and shoot to the buoy.

A singlehander can easily pick up a mooring. Lead a cleated bow line through the chock and outside all rigging to the cockpit. Pass by the mooring, and lean over from the cockpit to pick it up. Attach the line to the mooring, and drop it over the side.

DROPPING ANCHOR SINGLEHANDED One way for a singlehanded sailor to anchor is from the stern. Lower a spare anchor a few feet off the stern, and cleat it down. Run slowly downwind and, at the anchor spot, drop the stern anchor with plenty of scope until it bites in.

Or run the bow anchor and line outside all the standing rigging and allow it to hang over the stern. Tie the rode to a stern cleat with a slip knot. When the boat is at a stop over the anchoring spot, pull the slip knot and release the anchor. The anchor will bite in as the boat swings to its normal anchoring position.

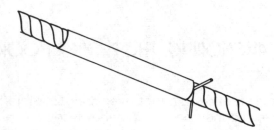

FIGURE 46

CHAFING GEAR Chafe is the worst enemy of a rope anchor rode. Use clear plastic tubing to protect the line. This tubing is difficult to keep in place because it tends to work down the line. Using a fid, open the line just below the chafing tube and insert a piece of light line. The protruding ends of this line will hold the chafing tube in place (see Figure 46).

If you are using anchor chain, strap a fender low on the bow to protect the topsides from being scratched by the chain.

A mooring buoy can also scuff up your topsides. Protect the hull by slipping an inner tube over the buoy.

CLEANING THE FOREDECK   To clean the foredeck after bringing a muddy chain and anchor on board, use a bucket of water attached to a lanyard. A bar of soap and a terry cloth towel can be kept in a net bag hanging in a clear area of the anchor locker.

Alternatively, run a hose from the galley salt-water spigot forward to clean the anchor and chain. A belt-driven pump run by the engine can be used for the same purpose.

CHAIN LOCKER   A great amount of destabilizing weight forward comes from the heavy anchor chain stored in the forepeak. Improve boat stability by leading the chain farther aft and below the water line. This can be accomplished by feeding it through a 4-inch PVC pipe to the desired location.

ANCHOR RODE   Splice a thimble to each end of the anchor rode so that it can be reversed periodically to minimize chafe.

Be sure that the bitter end of the rode is attached to a through-bolted connection on the boat's framework.

BOWSPRIT WINCH   By mounting a good-sized winch on the bowsprit, less strong members of the crew will be able to handle the anchor more easily.

CHAIN   Consider carrying half a dozen short lengths of extra chain as ballast. Shackling these sections together will give you strong additional chain to use as an all-chain anchor line in treacherous anchoring conditions.

When joining lengths of chain, use shackles with the lugs facing toward the boat. This will keep the lugs from catching as the chain feeds out.

If a chain does not lie straight, look for and replace elongated or cracked links.

ANCHOR CHAIN ENTRY HOLE   If you are taking green water over the bow, be sure to have prepared a way to close the anchor chain entry hole.

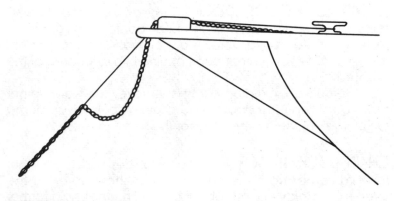

FIGURE 47

CHAIN PENDANT   To prevent the anchor chain from sawing away at the bobstay, attach a short length of line to the chain above the water line. Run the other end of the line to a bow cleat and put a strain on the line. The line will absorb the shocks, and the chain will sit quietly, not harming the bobstay (see Figure 47).

After dropping the anchor, don't forget to re-insert the cheek pin to keep the rode from jumping out of the roller as the boat yaws on the anchor.

Urethane rollers will give you the best wear if you use an anchor chain.

ANCHOR RODE WEIGHT   A taut anchor line is under great stress in rough seas. To reduce shock loads and improve yaw control, place a weight part way down the anchor line. The weight will help to distribute the load more evenly by giving added flexibility to the anchor line.

Create a weight by fitting a 20-pound sledgehammer head with an eye bolt and block. A messenger line fed

through the block allows the weight to be lowered and re-
trieved at will from the foredeck.

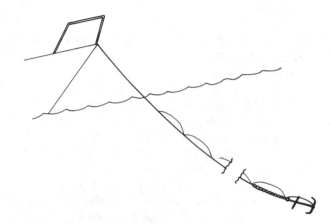

FIGURE 48

ANCHOR TRIPPING LINE   If the anchor is likely to become
fouled on the bottom, use a tripping line to aid in its retrieval.
A tripping line attached to the anchor crown will pull the anchor out by the flukes (see Figure 48).

There are various ways to attach a tripping line and have
it ready for use. For example, run a line from the crown of the
anchor to a surface float. Retrieve the float and give the tripping line a tug to release the anchor.

As an alternative, seize the tripping line to the anchor line
every 10 feet with breakable string. Pull on the tripping line,
breaking the string and tripping the anchor free.

To keep a loose tripping line from fouling on the rudder,
tie the deck end of the tripping line on the anchor rode a few
feet below the surface of the water. To retrieve, pull in the
anchor rode until you can get to the tripping line.

SECOND ANCHOR   If you anticipate heavy wind and
waves, put out two anchors on the same rode separated by
about 12 feet of chain.

DRAGGING ANCHOR   A good way to tell quickly if the anchor is dragging is to hold the rode in your hand. If the anchor is dragging, the rode will vibrate, and you will feel the anchor skip along the bottom.

FOULED ANCHOR   There are as many ways to get a fouled anchor up as there are ways to foul it in the first place. Try some of these ideas.

Pull the rode in as far as you can and let it go abruptly. The anchor may trip itself and come loose.

Pull the rode in as far as it will go, cleat it down taut, and let the wave action pull it out.

Pull as much of the rode out of the water as possible. Attach a line to the rode and hold on to the free end of the line. Release the rode. Now take the attached line out in the dinghy, and pull the anchor from the opposite direction.

Break the anchor loose by motoring in circles around the fouled anchor.

If two or more anchor ropes are fouled, ease out on the lowest rode and bring in the top line.

WINDLASS   An electric windlass will add tremendous power when you need to kedge off. Be sure to run the engine when using the electric windlass. It will cause a large power drain if you run it on battery alone.

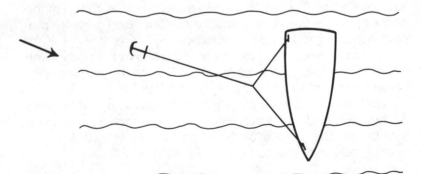

FIGURE 49

ANCHORING IN A SWELL   Improve the crew's comfort when riding at anchor by turning the bow into the swell and not into the wind. To get the boat to face the swell, run a line from a stern cleat and tie it taut to a point well forward of the bow on the anchor rode. This will form a bridle, putting the boat's nose into the swell (see Figure 49).

YAWING AT ANCHOR   Yawing is uncomfortable and puts unnecessary strain on the ground tackle. You can use several methods to minimize yawing.

Raise and sheet in the mizzen. If you have a single-masted boat, sheet in a small riding sail on the backstay.

If conditions permit, anchor the boat by the stern. This will effectively reduce hunting around the anchor.

Drop a second anchor when the boat is at the extreme limit of the yaw. Pay out its rode until the boat returns to its original position, and cleat down the second anchor line.

Boats with similar underwater configurations have similar swings and yaws. Therefore, to increase comfort and safety when you anchor in a crowded harbor, choose a spot near a boat of like design.

Occasionally, yawing can be lessened by dropping a small second anchor to the bottom. Each yaw will drag this anchor, thus reducing the swings.

SAILING OFF THE ANCHOR   There is nothing difficult about sailing off your anchor. With sails up, backwind the jib, fall off the wind, and sail away. If you fall off in the wrong direction, backwind the jib and the boat will come back into the wind.

If singlehanded, raise only the main and sheet it in hard. Leave the wheel free and go forward. Each time the main fills and the boat starts to sail, the anchor rode will pull it back into the wind to fall off again. Each time this happens, pull in as much rode as possible until you have pulled the anchor free.

SAILING OFF A MOORING   Pick up the mooring and walk it to the cockpit on the outside of the rigging. This will swing the boat stern to the wind. Detach the mooring line and sail off downwind.

LEAVING A RAFT UP   Leaving a raft up is more difficult than it looks. Use as many hands as you can muster to handle the lines. Slip out from the downwind side. If you leave to windward, the raft can break up.

MOORING VERSUS SLIP   The lower cost, the privacy, and the ease of docking at a mooring more than offset the inconveniences of rowing to shore and not having access to shore water and power. Additional advantages of anchoring in the open include fewer mosquitoes and more fresh air than are usually found at a slip.

ANCHOR DRAGGING ALARM   For added comfort at night, set the depth sounder alarm to ring if the boat drifts into shallow water.

POINTING SHIP   Pointing ship is a maneuver for turning your boat in her own length at anchor. To accomplish this, attach a line from the stern to the anchor rode forward. Haul in the stern line as you pay out the anchor rode. The boat will turn 180 degrees under your control. Attach the anchor rode to a stern cleat. You will now be stern to the wind for an easier departure or better ventilation.

KEDGING   When aground, kedging off with the anchor is often the only way to break free. Row the dinghy out to deep water and drop the kedging anchor. If you prefer, attach the anchor to a life jacket with light twine and swim the life jacket and anchor to the drop point. In either case, use the winch to pull the boat toward the anchor. (See also Going Aground page 114.)

DINGHY RODE   Flat braided polyester ribbon makes a good dinghy anchor line. It is extremely strong and comes wrapped around a reel that you can easily store in a small space in the dinghy.

ANCHORING A DINGHY OFF SHORE   Vandals and thieves make off with too many beached dinghys each year. Anchor the dinghy 30 feet off shore and make the job more difficult for them.

Tie a block to the top of the dinghy anchor. Run a long

line through the block and make both ends fast to the dinghy bow. Row part way to shore and drop anchor. Row the remaining way in to shore. Once on the beach, use the line to haul the dinghy back out to the anchor. Hide the shore end of the line and tie it fast. The dinghy will simply appear to be anchored off shore since the line connecting it to shore will be submerged under water.

LOOKING GOOD AT THE DOCK

The secrets of successful docking are anticipation and good contingency planning. Will there be an unexpected strong current? Could there be wind from a different direction at the dock? Is the crew ready for any sudden change in the docking plan?

As you near the dock, have a plan and an alternative in mind. Give each crewmember a station and a specific responsibility. Make ready docking lines and fenders. Prepare spring lines that create pivotal movements to control your final approach. With adequate forethought, docking can be a smooth operation. Many suggestions will follow to help you toward this end.

ENTERING A STRANGE HARBOR   Entering an unknown harbor without a chart calls all your senses and experience into play. Look at water color, observe the currents, watch the depth sounder, and go slowly.

Other boats of equivalent size docked at moorings or slips in the harbor indicate that a safe approach can be found.

The harbormaster is there to help and can be reached by radio.

DOWNWIND DOCKING   If docking downwind looks too tricky, turn into the wind just off the dock and drop the anchor and the sails. Pay out the anchor rode. This will slowly back you into the slip (see Figure 50). Secure the boat with docking lines. Leave the anchor out to help with departure unless it will present a hazard to other passing boats.

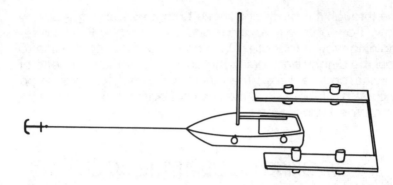

FIGURE 50

DOCKING UNDER SAIL   Come in under the main only. Approach as slowly as possible while still maintaining steering.

Push the boom into the wind as a brake if your approach under sail is too fast.

To come alongside a dock when the wind is blowing from the dock, approach the pier with main luffing and set a bow line. Pull the stern in with a spring line.

DOCKING UNDER POWER   To steer into a slip backward under power is often confusing because of the reverse response of the rudder. The whole process is made easier if you turn around facing the stern and steer normally.

LEE SIDE DOCKING   If the wind is blowing you away from the dock and there are only bow and stern lines out, motor forward slowly. This will pull the boat up to the dock. Quickly set spring lines to hold the boat in position. If you are docked with the engine off, save your strength and use the winch to bring the boat up to the pilings.

SINGLEHANDED DOCKING   A singlehander can dock best by using an endless loop docking line placed around a dock cleat or piling. When leaving, the singlehander need only to let go of one end of the line, remembering to pull it on board once clear of the dock.

MOVING THE BOAT AT THE DOCK Using the engine to reposition the boat in the slip is difficult. The boat can be moved more easily by someone on the dock pulling on the shrouds or by changing the docking line lengths and positions.

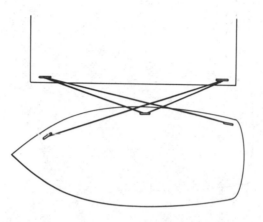

FIGURE 51

DOCKING LINES Lead long bow and stern lines aft and forward respectively, around a cleat or bollard. Then return each line to a center cleat on the boat. These two lines will work as spring lines as well as bow and stern lines (see Figure 51).

Splice a loop at the end of each dock line. Pull the standing part of the line through the loop, producing a large loop to throw over pilings and bollards.

BREAST LINE A breast line is a short piece of line attached midship to the dock bollard. It will hold the boat to the dock while you set other lines.

SPRING LINES When approaching a dock at an angle, put a line over a piling and cleat it at the bow. As you gradually move forward, the line will pull you into the dock. Use fenders to protect the topsides.

GOING THROUGH LOCKS With all lines and fenders ready, tie up to the windward wall of the lock. Use a stern line to attach to a bollard at the bow and a bow line for the stern bollard. Use endless loop lines for easy slipping at departure.

When going down in the lock, be sure to slack the lines as you descend.

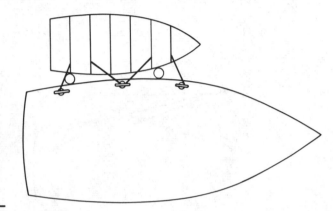

FIGURE 52

DINGHY AS TUG   A sailboat can be towed by a dinghy with an outboard. Tie the dinghy to the side of the sailboat with a line leading from the stern of the sailboat to the dinghy's bow (see Figure 52). The sailboat's rudder must be used to steer.

MANEUVERING AT SEA

This section discusses ideas for maneuvering at sea. Included are a number of good ideas to make sailing at night or in stormy seas safer and less frightening. Some thoughts on navigation are added especially for those times when your electronic aids fail and piloting must be done with instinct and personal skill alone.

BEATING INTO A STORM   Reefing the main to the maximum and running the engine allows you to slow the boat and sail high into the wind. This approach gives the best bow angle into the waves. Fall off to leeward after a large sea passes to prevent going straight into the trough behind the wave. Watch the engine instruments to avoid overheating.

By moving the lead blocks aft, tightening the halyard, and sheeting the storm jib in as far as possible, you can reduce the jib's driving strength.

DOWNWIND IN A STORM Steering downwind in a storm is difficult and requires full attention. Under some conditions the rudder may actually stall. To regain control, turn the rudder back and forth as quickly as possible.

There are known difficulties associated with using a conventional drogue to reduce boat speed. Recent evidence shows that the new nylon ribbon drogue is an effective alternative and can slow the boat to 2 to 3 knots. It does not create heavy shock loads when the boat accelerates on a wave, and it is easier to retrieve than the conventional variety. If you don't have a ribbon drogue, try trailing long lines attached to a stern bight.

PASSING ANOTHER BOAT DOWNWIND If you must pass very near another boat while going downwind, be upwind of her. Should there be a problem, you can more quickly come into the wind or luff than you can fall off or jibe.

RAISE JIB DOWNWIND When you are going downwind, there is less apparent wind and heel. Take advantage of this flat, quiet situation and set the jib going downwind. It will fill easily, out ahead of the boat, away from the foredeck crew.

WING AND WING When winging out the jib, keep the pole parallel to the boom.

SENSE WIND DIRECTION ON A RUN Wet the back of your neck to better feel a soft wind when on a downwind run.

STORMPROOF THE ENGINE If you are not using the engine in heavy weather, close the engine through-the-hull fittings to keep water out of the manifold. Leave a note in a conspicuous place to remind yourself to open the fittings when the weather clears.

HEAVING TO
In moderate storm conditions, it may be preferable to heave to in order to improve deck conditions while changing to storm sails.

When the time comes to heave to, select the tack at which the boat rides most comfortably. Come about, keeping the jib sheeted to the windward side. Let the main out and lash the wheel to leeward. The boat will slow considerably and drift downwind in slick water.

NIGHT SAILING
When you first see a light, lower your eye a few inches to judge its distance. If the light disappears, it is near its maximum visible range.

Timed too soon, a distant signal light may give a false sequence by dipping down occasionally between wave crests.

Depth perception is confusing in the dark. When you are nearing the shore at night, it's easy to assume that you are closer than you are.

If you see a light's reflection on the water, you are within a few hundred yards of the light.

As another boat approaches, line its lights up with two of your shrouds. If after a few minutes they are in the same position, you are on a potential collision course.

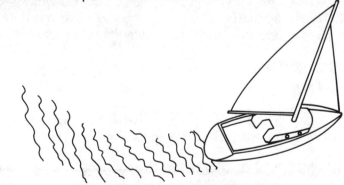

FIGURE 53

CURRENT AND TIDES Current is difficult to see except in relation to something else. For example, current can be easily discerned if there is a buoy to observe.

Wind blowing against a current will cause easily identified choppy water.

You can usually tell if you are making leeway as a result of current or of tide by seeing if your wake runs straight. A current will set your wake off to the side. The angle between the boat's centerline and the off-center wake indicates the amount of leeway (see Figure 53).

OBSERVE WAVES Much can be learned from constant observation of nearby waves. Wave patterns change when the bottom shelves off or when you near a reef. The direction of waves usually indicates wind direction.

Avoid the crests of choppy, undisciplined waves. Try to sail through the smoothest part of waves rather than confront the crests head on.

HEAVY WEATHER PILOTING NEAR SHORE Use all your senses when piloting in unfamiliar waters. Observe the water conditions, watch for signs of land and changes in smells. Compare depth soundings to the chart. At night, look for city lights reflecting off clouds.

When making an uncertain landfall, intentionally err to one side of your destination. Then, when you sight land, there will be no doubt which way to turn.

NAVIGATING WITHOUT INSTRUMENTS If all instruments fail, you can still navigate using common sense and old sea lore.

The sun reaches a bearing of due south at exactly noon when it is at its highest point in the sky. On a moving deck, it is difficult to determine the highest point, but it can be estimated quite closely. Once you know where south is located, you can steer in any direction.

Another way to find south is to orient yourself so that the hour hand of your wristwatch is directed at the sun. The point halfway between twelve o'clock and the hour hand is south.

RADIO NAVIGATION   Radio direction finders are not as accurate as other navigation devices. When you think you are getting close to a beacon, veer off to the side. If the radio bearing shows a radical change, you are close. If there is a very small change, you are still far away.

By marking aeronautical radio beacons on your chart, you can use these very powerful signals for navigation.

RADAR NAVIGATION   Ship's radar can be used for many applications.

You can spot crossing situations to avoid collisions.

When you are hove to, radar can show the effect of current and drift on your position.

To get a fix in a fog, identify the distance to a fixed object on the radar screen. Locate this object on the chart, and draw an arc at this distance from the object. Take a compass bearing to the object. The point at which the arc crosses your bearing is a fix.

You can see heavy rain squalls on the radar screen.

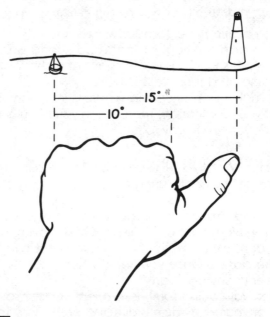

FIGURE 54

ESTIMATING SPEED It is possible to estimate speed without a knotmeter. Mark the time that it takes a wood chip or wad of paper dropped off the bow to reach the stern. Boat speed can be calculated as the length of the boat, divided by 1.67, multiplied by the time in seconds.

Taffrail logs towed behind the boat give very accurate speed and distance information.

ESTIMATING BEARINGS A good way to estimate a bearing is to make a fist and stretch your arm out in front of you. The width of your four knuckles will be about 10 degrees. By also sticking out your thumb, it will increase to 15 degrees (see Figure 54).

COMPASS ADJUSTMENT Always use a nonmagnetic screwdriver when adjusting the compass. A magnetized one could push the compass over the deep end.

COMPASS ACCURACY When chartering a boat, you can't be sure of compass accuracy. Make some comparisons by using a hand-held compass to take readings from a spot on the boat that is least affected by metal objects. Compare your readings with the main compass. Loran can also be used to verify compass accuracy.

Each spring you should use this technique to check your main compass. Motor in at least six headings, comparing the hand-held compass with the main compass. Be sure to turn off the motor to check that the readings don't change.

$$T = 310° \qquad W = +$$
$$V = \quad 9°E \qquad E = -$$
$$M = 301°$$
$$D = \quad 5°W$$
$$C = 306°$$

FIGURE 55

COMPASS CORRECTION Use the TVMDC rule to apply deviation and variation corrections to true degree headings. In a column, enter the true (T) compass heading, the variation (V), the magnetic heading (M), and the compass deviation (D). Add or subtract the values as you proceed to calculate the accurate compass (C) heading (see Figure 55).

CELESTIAL NAVIGATION The U.S. Government Printing Office, Washington, DC 20402, has the *Nautical Almanac* available on a computer disk. It is a great source of data for helping the homebound winter sailor to practice celestial navigation. Very few boats have an on-board computer, but for those that do, the almanac disk is a real space saver.

STAR IDENTIFICATION Polaris, or the North Star, is a basic key to star identification. It is the star at the end of the Little Dipper's handle. Look north at an elevation that is the same as your latitude to find Polaris. Conversely, you can estimate your latitude by measuring Polaris's elevation.

WINDVANES Windvanes can be a boon to the cruising sailor. However, exercise great caution if you are alone in the cockpit. Should you fall over the side, the boat will continue to sail on, leaving you in the water with little chance of reboarding. Wearing a safety harness is the solution when sailing alone with a windvane.

TRANSFERRING PASSENGERS AT SEA There is no completely safe way to transfer passengers at sea. If it is essential to do so, put the passengers into the dinghy and tow the dinghy behind the forward boat. Bring the second sailboat alongside the dinghy. The people can now be transferred with reasonable safety from the dinghy (see Figure 56).

KEEPING A WEATHER EYE

For ages, man has been trying to predict the weather. Quite effective scientific methods are used today. By becoming

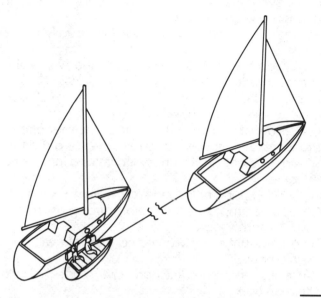

FIGURE 56

a keen observer of nature, however, you can predict if change is on the way. Using techniques applicable to the northern hemisphere (the southern hemisphere is usually the opposite), some handy methods of simple forecasting are given in this chapter. And don't lose sight of the old sailors' weather rhymes—they generally hold quite true.

WEATHER SENSE   Save yourself from blundering into bad weather by maintaining a conscious weather check. Keep a weather log on wind change, cloud change, wave direction, barometer readings, and regular radio weather checks. Be particularly aware of weather patterns for the few days before a cruise. Knowing what to expect may help to determine your route and destination.

WEATHER LORE   Sailors for ages have been using practical weather lore with surprising accuracy. There are good reasons why men at sea listen to sayings such as "Red sky at night, sailors delight; Red sky in the morning, sailors take warning."

Weather follows fairly well-defined rules that validate these observations. Here are some others.

Weather in the northern hemisphere usually runs from west to east.

Today's weather 400 to 500 miles to the west will often be tomorrow's weather here.

The lower, the darker, and the faster storm clouds approach, the worse the storm will be.

Thunderstorms usually occur late in a summer afternoon.

A strong first wind followed by rain predicts a short storm. Rain first with wind afterward usually indicates a long period of stormy weather.

Long buildup, long hold; short forewarning, soon past.

If the weather improves too rapidly after a storm, look for another low to come soon.

A halo around the moon predicts that rain will begin in about twelve hours.

Storm clouds that build into an anvil shape will bring a storm within an hour.

As you stand with your back to the wind, look at the high clouds. If they come from your left, expect poor weather. If they come from the right, the weather will be all right. If they are running parallel to the surface winds, there will be little change for the next four to six hours.

You can often expect brief violent weather after a low has passed and the barometer begins to rise very rapidly.

TAPE WEATHER FORECAST Record radio weather forecasts on a portable tape recorder to replay at a later time when you are making navigation decisions. There are bound to be comments you missed the first time. Listening to a series of forecasts will clearly show weather progression over a period.

WEATHER ALERT RADIOS Weather alert radios are available through many marine catalogs and stores. These special radios sound a ten-second warning signal and flash a red light when the National Weather Service sounds its emergency signal.

RADIO STATIC   An approaching lightning storm will cause intense static on a low-frequency AM radio station.

BAROMETER READINGS   If you are expecting a weather change, make note of the barometer reading every few hours. At the same time, keep track of surface wind directions.
The more rapid the barometric change, the more intense and immediate the storm will be. Around the continental United States, the following wind direction and barometer readings suggest specific weather trends:
A falling barometer with wind from the east or northeast indicates a storm in twelve to twenty-four hours from the south or southwest.
A falling barometer with a south or southeast wind indicates a storm approaching from the west or northwest within twelve to twenty-four hours.

FRONTS AND CLOUDS   Weather is most violent where fronts meet. Look at high clouds for indications of weather change. High cirrus clouds with one edge turned up show wind direction. These are messenger clouds for an approaching front. The winds will veer clockwise as the front passes.
As a warm front ensues, high cirrus clouds will be followed by veil-like cirro-stratus clouds that make halos around the moon and sun. Poor weather becomes more certain as dark, thick alto-stratus clouds begin to obscure the sun. Wind and rain will soon follow.
On a hot summer day, low cumulus clouds do not threaten rain. Cumulus clouds must go to a very high altitude to form ice crystals and produce rain.

WARM AND COLD FRONTS   One of the basic patterns of weather is that a high pressure area will flow toward a nearby low. Fair weather is most often found in and ahead of a high pressure front. Bad or unsettled weather will be found in a low pressure area. The most severe weather is most often at the leading edge of a frontal system.

WEATHER MAP ISOBARS   On a weather map, closely spaced isobars indicate strong winds whereas widely separated isobars show light and variable winds.

Obtain from NOAA, Room 6013, Department of Commerce, Washington, D.C. 20230 a copy of *Explanation of the Daily Weather Map*. This publication will explain all symbols used on weather maps.

FIGURE 57

WIND PREDICTION   Put your back to the wind on a port tack. A low pressure system will be located in the direction of your extended left arm. On a starboard tack, face your body 45 degrees to the right of the wind, and extend your left arm to point at the low (see Figure 57).

A falling barometer and easterly winds are a prelude to bad weather. A rising barometer and winds changing from the west predict fair and clear weather.

Stable weather is accompanied by light morning winds increasing to their strongest by about midday when air temperature is also at its highest.

Many scattered clouds often indicate variable winds. If the sky is clearing of clouds, you can expect steady winds.

To calculate the actual wind speed of a reported Beaufort wind scale number, multiply the wind force number by 6 and subtract 10.

PREDICTING FOG   There are often early indicators that predict fog. Look for a fuzziness around lights, smoke rising very slowly, water temperature colder than air temperature, or a hazy white sky with a poorly defined horizon. Other indicators are a steady offshore wind and increasing humidity.

If there is no weather change predicted and you have fog today, expect fog tomorrow.

When the relative humidity reaches 100 percent, consider the strong possibility of fog.

When the spread between the dew point and the air temperature is but a few points, fog is a probability. Test for the dew point with a psychrometer.

Fog will begin to dissipate with increasing wind and temperature. The same will occur when the wind shifts from an onshore to offshore wind.

PILOTING IN FOG   If you are the bow lookout in fog, occasionally close your eyes and concentrate on all the sounds and smells to gather additional locational clues. Cup your hands around your ears to direct your hearing zone.

Range your eyes along the horizon and look for darker shapes or even a white curl at the near horizon. This curl could be another boat's bow wave.

If approaching a shoreline under power, stop the engine and have the lookout shout. An echo could signal a raised shoreline close by. Land smells, changes in water color, or a steeper wave pattern may indicate your proximity to shore.

To locate your position on a chart, use your last good fix as a starting point. Take frequent depth readings until you find a series of readings that coincide with a depth curve on the chart. Follow that depth curve until you reach a known mark to establish a new navigational fix.

CHAPTER 6

~~~

SHIPS' SYSTEMS

Previous chapters have addressed topics concerned with all parts of the boat except the systems that run it. This part of the book presents ideas covering the engine, electronics, and electricity.

The first section discusses the engine, drive chain, and propeller. Effective maintenance of this system is a high priority for most sailors.

The second section addresses onboard electronics. Most electronic devices for the boat are getting more compact and less costly every year, making them more accessible to the average sailor.

Finally, the last section touches on electricity—particularly power converters, solar panels, water driven charging systems, and shore power hookups. Although boats can sail perfectly well without electricity, the loss of convenience and safety in the absence of electricity on board would be considerable.

THE ENGINE: THE ALTERNATIVE POWER SOURCE

Most sailors own their boats to enjoy the pleasures of sailing. There are, however, times when the engine is needed. There are days without wind. There are difficult docking situations. And there are times when you must quickly get to your destination in fluky winds. Purists sail without engines. However, having an engine is a big help toward satisfactory cruising, no matter what your aesthetics may be.

Unfortunately, sailboat engines can be noisy, smelly, capricious, and expensive to maintain. These unwanted characteristics of the engine and its auxiliary parts, the drive train and the electrical components can be controlled, however. The following ideas will help you to bring these beasts under control.

QUIET A NOISY ENGINE   There are things you can do to eliminate vibration and unnecessary engine noise.

First make sure that the engine is properly aligned. Then cushion it on solid rubber blocks.

Install a constant velocity joint between the transmission and the propeller shaft. A 15-degree range of movement and greatly reduced shaft vibration will be achieved with this flexible joint.

The exhaust pipe, fuel lines, and instrument cables should also have flexible connections.

An air cleaner will act as a muffler on the engine.

Much sound and heat will be contained if you cover the engine room walls with 2-inch thick foam that has been lined with foil. Foam-backed carpet can be used as an alternative lining.

ENGINE ROOM   Attach a copy of the engine operating instructions to the engine room bulkhead using a piece of clear contact paper (see Figure 58).

Hang your oil can in a piece of PVC pipe that has been attached to the engine room bulkhead.

Get a trouble light with a large end clamp and 50 feet of cord. The end clamp allows you to attach the lamp almost anywhere to shed lots of light on an engine repair area.

Keep a roll of paper towels on a rack in the engine room to clean up spills.

Keep the engine clean, and it will be easier to see leaks when they occur.

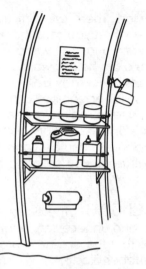

FIGURE 58

Store cans of oil, filters, tools, and fan belts in the engine room on shelves easily placed between the ribs of the bulkhead.

BATTERIES Cover batteries with securely fastened, waterproof containers that will prevent a short circuit in case of engine room flooding. This cover can be a plastic pan strapped over the battery like a diving bell. The cover must leave an air space around the bottom of the battery so that gas can escape (see Figure 59). Should the battery area be flooded, the cover will keep air within and water out.

When starting the engine, turn battery switch to ALL. When at anchor, cycle between battery 1 and battery 2 on odd and even days respectively.

Don't depend on the electric panel voltmeter to determine your battery's condition. Check each battery cell with a hydrometer.

To transport a battery more easily, use a battery carrying strap that can be purchased at an auto supply store.

A clean battery will give noticeably improved performance. Clean tops and sides with weak detergent and water or with ammonia, then rinse off. It has even been said that cola

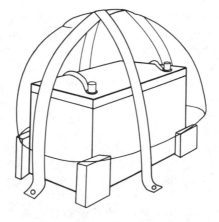

FIGURE 59

drinks will clean battery tops. Be sure to temporarily close the vent plugs with toothpicks while you clean.

Burnish the battery terminals with a terminal cleaner or wire brush and coat with a light spray of WD-40.

Periodically check the battery condition with a voltmeter. Typical battery voltmeter readings (for a 12-volt battery) are:

11.2 volts is a dead battery.

12.2 volts is a low battery.

13.8 volts is a full charge from a battery charger.

14.4 volts is a full charge from the alternator.

Don't leave marine batteries too long with a partial charge. If they are to be left unused for a long period, be sure to leave them fully charged.

FAN BELTS   Black powdery residue found nearby indicates that belts are wearing and should be replaced. The occurrence of wear will be reduced if you make sure that pulleys are in line and tension is correct.

TEMPORARY ENGINE GASKET   Silicone rubber sealant will suffice as a temporary engine gasket.

OIL CHANGE   When changing the oil, keep the boat and yourself clean by using an oil vacuum pump, available at auto supply stores. First run the engine to warm the oil. Then insert the hose into the dipstick hole and pump. Pumping creates suction that will draw out the engine oil. Let the oil flow into a plastic bag in a bucket. Afterward, clean out the pump by running some diesel fuel through it. The same procedure can be performed by using a rotary pump driven by an electric drill.

To change the oil without a pump, try the following procedure. Use rubber bands to attach a plastic bag to one end of a vegetable can from which you have removed both top and bottom. After removing the engine drain plug, put the open end of the can under the drain to catch all the oil in the plastic bag.

Another way to contain oil is to buy a box of absorbent gravel-like material that will hold up to 5 quarts of oil and is marketed for this specific purpose. Five to 10 pounds of cat litter or sweeping compound in a garbage bag will accomplish the same objective.

DRIP PAN   A large drip pan under the engine will catch all oil drips and keep them out of the bilge. A smaller pan can be held under the filter to catch oil when changing either the filter or the oil.

USING THE ENGINE AS A BILGE PUMP   In an extreme emergency, the engine can be used to pump the bilge. Permanently install a T-fitting on the engine water intake hose. Attach another hose to the second outlet on the T-fitting. Place the end of this hose, which has been fitted with a fine strainer, into the bilge. To use, turn the T-valve and run the engine to pump the bilge. Use this procedure with extreme care else all sorts of strange items could be drawn into the engine.

DIESEL FILTERS   Sediment will eventually settle on the bottom of the fuel tank and can get mixed into the fuel by the movement of the boat. Try to eliminate dirt by installing double fuel filters.

If you must clean out the tank, use a hand pump with a long extension to reach the bottom of the tank. Pump until clear fuel is being removed.

DIESEL ENGINE CARE   The best medicine for a diesel engine is prevention.

Change oil every 100 hours.

Buy fuel from high-volume dealers. Do not buy home heating oil.

Ether and other additives are not necessary if the engine is well maintained.

Replace filters regularly.

ASSURE DRY DIESEL FUEL   It is imperative to keep water out of diesel fuel. Centrifugal filters are on the market that actually spin unwanted water out and away from the fuel.

DIESEL ENGINE TROUBLESHOOTING   If a diesel will not start, the problem is most often in the fuel system. If air in the fuel line appears to be the problem, open the bleed screws on the engine until solid fuel comes out.

If you suspect that there is water in the fuel, take a sample of fuel near the bottom of the tank and examine it for water. If you find water, completely drain the tank. If the fuel seems okay, change the fuel filter.

Check for overheating caused by a restriction in the cooling system. Clean strainers, inspect the belt on the water pump, and make sure you don't have a fouled prop.

Next, check the oil level. If it is adequate, try to start the engine again.

If the starter works but the engine does not start, you may need to replace the glow plug.

UNIDENTIFIED ENGINE NOISE   If there is an engine noise you cannot locate, use an inexpensive stethoscope. Touch the disc to various engine parts to find the troublesome internal noise. Old-time mechanics put a wrench end against the bone behind their ear and then touch the wrench to the engine. Watch your hair and clothing if you attempt this.

TROUBLESHOOTING A GAS ENGINE   If the engine will not catch, consider fuel supply, compression, and ignition as possible sources of trouble.

The fuel supply should be checked at the fuel pump, at the fuel pump filter, and at the fuel lines.

If compression is the problem, you will need a mechanic.

If ignition is the problem, check the points, the spark plug gap, and all wire connections.

POINTS If you are going to operate the engine in cold weather, keep a light bulb of low wattage burning near the distributor while you are off the boat. The light bulb will keep moisture from condensing on the points, and the engine will be easier to start.

ALTERNATORS The alternator is one of the weak links in the engine electrical system. Consider installing two alternators and regulators for redundancy. A double-pole, double-throw switch can direct the current from the chosen alternator. Remember to remove the positive wire from the regulator of the disabled alternator before switching over.

When an alternator is not charging, the problem can often be traced to a wire loosened by vibration or a loose belt. Also check the positive output wire for potential corrosion.

LIGHT BULBS The damp, salt air environment on the boat may cause light bulb bases to corrode in the socket. Protect the bulb by lightly coating its base with petroleum jelly before inserting it into the light socket.

FUEL LINES Clamp fuel lines in place so that they do not chafe or lie against a hot engine part.

SHAFT BRAKE Fashion a shaft brake by using a pair of vise-grip pliers locked on the shaft and positioned so that when the shaft turns, the pliers will jam against the hull (see Figure 60). This will prevent the propeller from turning while you are sailing.

STUFFING BOX To determine whether the stern gland is properly adjusted, run the engine for about a half hour. If the

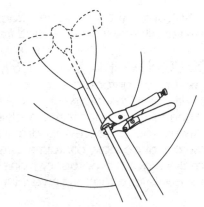

FIGURE 60

stern gland is not too hot to handle and it does not leak, then the adjustment is proper.

EXHAUST SYSTEM Prevent water from running back into the manifold through the water intake by looping the exhaust system hose 3 feet above the waterline. For further insurance, put a stop-valve behind the muffler.

PROPELLERS When you choose a propeller, it is the amount of torque, not the engine horsepower, that should be your main consideration.

A two-bladed prop has less drag than a three-bladed one. However, if you motor frequently, a three-bladed prop will deliver better performance.

For racing, a folding prop reduces drag measurably but is the least efficient of all for motoring.

Recently advertised in sailing magazines is a knife-like gadget that attaches to the propeller shaft and shreds plastic sheeting, cuts ropes, and helps to keep the prop from fouling. It will, however, add somewhat to underwater drag.

Keep the prop blades clean by wiping them with STP or a similar product.

OIL STORAGE Oil is normally packaged in quart size, spiral wound fiber cans that often leak when they are abused. Store your spare oil cans in plastic beverage trays used to carry quart soda bottles. The cans will be protected from damage, and the storage area or bilge will be protected from leaking oil.

FUNNELS FOR LIQUIDS   Funnels are nearly essential when adding oil or fuel to an outboard engine on a rocking boat. Select funnels with large reservoirs, filter screens, and flexible neck spouts. Funnels that support themselves give you two free hands. Always be prepared to drain the supposedly empty funnel into a disposable container after use.

You can make a good emergency funnel from the upper half of a bleach bottle or a rubber glove with a finger cut out.

HIGH TECH ELECTRONICS AT SEA

Most electronics on the boat are related to either radio or navigation equipment. There is, however, a growing interest in having computers, stereo systems, and cellular telephones on board. With an increasing number of choices, there is an enormous selection of electronic equipment available for use on the boat.

VHF RADIOS   VHF has been a communication wonder for years. The newer compact portable VHFs are even more versatile because they can go with you to shore, into the dinghy, or even up the mast.

VHF ANTENNAS   Carefully select your VHF antenna. Because it works on line of sight, you should consider its wave pattern. If you mount the antenna at the top of the mast, it should have a broad wave pattern to compensate for the heel of the boat. Transmissions will be lost if the antenna is pointed down into the water or up to the sky. An antenna that is mounted lower will not be as sensitive to heel but will lose line of sight distance. Here, you should have a long-distance wave pattern with a narrower band.

Minimize the number of antennas at the top of the mast by using the Loran antenna to receive VHF.

Make sure that the lower insulator of a backstay VHF antenna is high enough to be out of accidental reach.

EMERGENCY ANTENNA   An emergency antenna has to be the correct length for its specific frequency. Calculate the length in inches by dividing 462 by the frequency in megahertz.

RADIO INTERFERENCE   There are many potential sources of radio interference on the boat. These include fluorescent lights, small DC motors, alternators, radar, Loran, depth sounder, and ignition system. Use a portable AM radio to zero in on the exact source of interference. Static will be strongest as you approach the cause of the problem.

The sounds you hear on the radio can give you a clue to the interference source. A popping sound probably indicates the spark plugs. A whirring sound usually identifies the alternator as the culprit. An irregular clicking sound is generally caused by an electromechanical relay. Scratchy sounds that occur when the starter is used logically indicate the starter as the cause of radio interference.

A homemade interference detector can be made from a 1-microfarad, 200-volt capacitor. Put alligator clips on the end of each capacitor lead wire. Ground one clip and touch the other to the piece of equipment suspected of causing interference. If this results in a low noise level, attach a permanent capacitor.

Several measures that can prevent radio interference include installing resistive spark plugs, grounding the coil, cleaning and tightening all connections, and putting a bypass capacitor on the positive terminal of the ignition coil.

Radio and navigation equipment that operates near 50 kilohertz requires noise suppressors of the following types: 5A-50 volt ignition filters at the source of interference on electronic ignitions, and 70A-50 volt filters on the alternator.

The autopilot can be affected by interference when radio signals are being transmitted. Therefore, check the autopilot during transmission to determine if it is operating properly.

HAM AND SINGLE SIDE BAND (SSB) RADIOS   A relatively new innovation is the automatic print capability of ham and

SSB radios. A properly equipped radio unit will receive and print messages, freeing the operator from monitoring the radio channels at prescribed times.

SHORTWAVE RADIO A shortwave radio has a definite place on the boat. It can receive worldwide entertainment, weather, news, and broadcasts from other ships. Even more important, WWV and WWVH give continuous time checks, predictions on the quality of radio transmissions for the next six hours, and updates on sea conditions and wind strength.

STEREO It is extremely pleasant to have stereo music on the boat. This can be accomplished by using good-quality automobile stereo equipment or one of the numerous models made specifically for the marine environment.

Stereo speakers mounted in the wall produce improved bass resonance because of the effect of the hollow bulkhead. However, flush-mounted speaker boxes provide added versatility. Store extra wire behind them so that the speakers can be brought up on deck.

Keep cassette tapes stored in an insulated food container. By being in a cool, dark, dry environment, the tape life will be extended.

If you need better reception, attach a car antenna to the radio. Extend the antenna to 31 inches for FM stations and full extension for AM stations. A splitter could be attached to a masthead antenna for even better FM reception.

If you choose to connect a CD player, shock mount it to keep it from being jolted and harmed.

Use coaxial wires to prevent radio interference.

Boat wiring is double wire. Therefore, you should lead the radio ground wire to the negative terminal on the electrical panel or battery, not to a ground.

COMPUTERS Small battery-operated, lap-top computers are finding a place on the boat. Keep the computer covered to prevent condensation and salt from getting into the circuitry.

There are numerous functions a computer can perform besides entertainment. Create a maintenance log on the computer that includes a calendar of tasks, location of parts on the boat, and specific maintenance procedures. Enter descriptive information about your favorite destinations, including compass bearings, Loran coordinates, and exact spots to anchor. If you have a printer, you can make a hard copy of navigational data to include in the chart folder in the cockpit.

AUTOPILOTS   More and more autopilots are being used today in crowded waters. Collisions can easily occur if the autopilot is unattended under these conditions. If you encounter heavy boat traffic, either be on constant lookout or take the helm.

When you are shorthanded on the boat, an autopilot lets you stand lookout at the bow or quickly do another task without having to worry about maintaining course. Remember to use a safety harness if you are alone on the boat while using the autopilot.

It is easier to see the autopilot windvane at night if you apply some reflective tape to the vane.

KNOTMETERS   Place the knotmeter transducer beneath the waterline, forward of midship and below the turn of the bilge. This is the site of least turbulence and produces the most accurate readings.

Current can affect your knotmeter speed reading. If you think the reading may be inaccurate, verify it by sailing in reciprocal directions and averaging the two speeds.

DEPTH FINDER   The accuracy of your depth sounder can be determined by comparing lead line depths to depth sounder readings. A lead line can be used only while the boat is drifting slowly.

RADIO DIRECTION FINDER (RDF)   When piloting near shore with an RDF, use low-frequency stations below 850 kilohertz. These can be tuned in more accurately than stations of a higher frequency.

CELLULAR TELEPHONES   Cellular telephones are increasingly being used on boats, particularly by those who already have one in their car. Because both car and boat run on 12-

volt systems, you need only install a mount on the boat to be able to transfer the phone. A masthead antenna will improve transmission and reception.

Compared to VHF, these phones are static free, more private, and legal to use for business and private conversations.

Because cellular telephone messages are not monitored by the Coast Guard, they cannot be relied on for emergency situations.

If you have a computer on board, the addition of a modem will allow the transfer of data.

ELECTRICITY, KEEPING IT BRIGHT

Electrical installation and maintenance are very basic and are covered at length in electrical manuals. There are, however, some specific differences and precautions to be noted when handling electricity in a marine environment. A few of these ideas follow in this last section.

ELECTRICAL SCHEMATICS   Particularly after you have bought a used boat, it will be worth your time to trace all the boat's wiring and produce a schematic drawing to be included in the maintenance log.

12-VOLT TO 120-VOLT POWER CONVERTERS   There are various ways to run 120-volt appliances and equipment on the boat.

Use an engine-driven or portable gasoline AC generator to power the appliances.

Use an inverter to turn DC battery current into AC current. You can do this by attaching jumper cables from a 12-volt battery to a 1,200-watt inverter.

SOLAR PANELS   Strategically placed solar panels designed for use on boats can provide enough amperage to maintain a trickle charge on a seldom used battery.

Multiple solar units can actually produce enough electricity to power small appliances.

WATER-DRIVEN CHARGING SYSTEMS   An adequate speed for a water-driven charging system to produce a usable amount of electricity is 4 to 6 knots. There are three ways to use a free-wheeling propeller to produce electricity. In each system, the propeller is connected through a generator to the batteries. Be sure to use a voltage regulator to prevent overcharging the batteries.

Disconnect a variable pitch propeller from the engine by using a dog clutch. The turning propeller will now activate the generator to produce electric current.

Attach a separate prop to the stern. This will serve the same function without detaching the engine prop.

Last, consider a towed water generator.

WIRING   Run wiring through PVC pipe of a small diameter for improved safety and aesthetics.

Don't use wire nuts or twist caps. If possible, solder all the electrical connections on a boat. After soldering, insulate the terminal with a short piece of clear heat-shrink tubing. Don't use electrical tape.

An alternative to soldering is to use a variable size crimping tool to permanently attach terminals to the wire.

Electrical wires located near the compass should be twisted around each other to prevent electrical interference with the compass.

Use stranded wire. Solid wire will eventually flex too often and break.

Select a larger size wire if you have any question about which size to use.

EXTENSION CORDS   Rather than using a long extension cord that must be coiled for storage, choose one of the flexible "slinky" style cords. It will stretch a great distance but store in a small space.

When using an extension cord with shore power, remember to support the cord so that it does not go into the water.

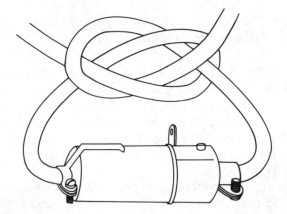

FIGURE 61

If you connect two cords, tie them in a square knot at the connection to keep them from pulling apart (see Figure 61).

AC SHORE POWER   Ground fault interrupters should be installed on your AC shore power system to automatically shut down the electricity whenever there is a short in the wiring.

Add up all the amperage from the lights and equipment on the boat. You should have circuit breakers rated at 75 percent of this total amperage.

CHAPTER 7

~~~

CRUISING

Up until now we have dealt with the mechanics of managing the boat. Let's now look at other factors that can increase your cruising pleasure. This part of the book looks into onboard entertainment, shoreside activities, children, pets, and the importance of the dinghy. Good planning in these areas can make or break a successful cruise.

LEISURE: SAILING IN COMFORT

LEISURE EVENTS   There is an almost endless variety of activities possible during your cruise. Try fishing, crabbing, snorkeling, biking, hiking, surfboarding, and skateboarding. For the less hardy, try reading books, listening to cassette tapes, cooking, ropework, and macrame. Raise cactus, ferns, or hydroponic gardens. Collect shells, pebbles, and stamps. Wile away the hours with board games and cards. Play a guitar, harmonica, or kazoo to provide musical entertainment. Tape all your favorite records from home for hours of great stereo listening on the boat. This may be the perfect occasion to take a correspondence course while you have idle time.

FLYING KITES   Kite flying from the stern of the boat is great fun for kids. The additional wind effect gained by the moving boat is often enough to raise a kite on days with little wind. Long plastic dragon kites, exotic Chinese kites, or high-performance geometric designs make it even more of a challenge.

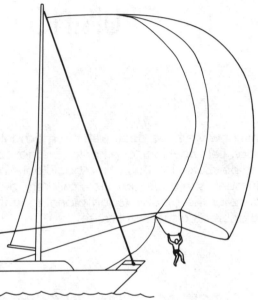

FIGURE 62

SPINNAKER FLYING   For spinnaker flying, the sailboat must be anchored from the stern, preferably using a bridle to keep the boat steady. Tie a line from the spinnaker tack to the clew, allowing it to droop 15 feet longer than the distance across the bottom of the sail. Attach a trip line to either the tack or the clew. Hoist the sail and let it fly loose. The swimmer in the water can now grab the drooping line, filling the spinnaker. Off they will go, ahead of the boat. Pull the trip line when your flying crewmember wants to take a plunge. Keep the crew's safety as your first priority when spinnaker flying (see Figure 62).

SAILBOARDS   Having a sailboard along on your cruise can be wonderful fun, but handling and storing it safely on deck present a problem. Try attaching it to a padded stanchion by tying a line through the daggerboard.

Put a towing eye in the bow of the sailboard for tying up during a change of riders or for towing behind the sailboat on calm days.

PHONE HOME When you go on an extended cruise, take along your address book. You never know whom you might want to call.

PARTY TIME Attach a bright colored light to the forestay on the night of your party. In a crowded marina, it will make your boat easy to find.

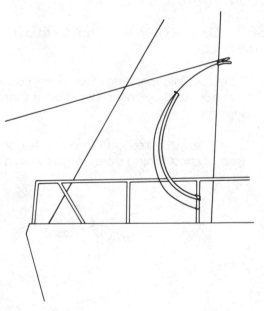

FIGURE 63

FISHING AT SEA A good method for fishing on the surface is to troll a multihooked yellow lure at above 4 knots. Use 100 feet of 40-pound-test line with little or no weight. Tie the line to a stanchion. Attach one end of surgical tubing 10 feet long to the same stanchion. Attach the other end to the fishing line 10 feet out. Now clip the fishing line at about head height to a nearby shroud, using a clothespin (see Figure 63). The surgical tubing will absorb the initial shock as the fish hits and pulls the line away from the clothespin.

Using much the same technique as above, fish deep below the surface for mackerel. Locate the mackerel by watching for seagulls feeding. One successful technique is to troll with 300 feet of 100-pound-test line, six or seven feathered hooks, and a 2-pound weight. Another rig is a line with a swivel and 2-pound weight connected to 12 feet of nylon line ending with a swivel, spinner, and hook. Paravanes can be used instead of a heavy weight to drive the hook down.

HOOK GUARDS   Protect the fisherman from getting jabbed by a hook in the tackle box by wrapping the hooks in aluminum foil or sticking them to a magnet.

ROD HOLDER   Clamp a fishing rod holder to a stanchion at the stern of the boat.

KILLING FISH   By carefully pressing your thumb and two fingers into a fish's mouth and pulling its head back sharply, it can be dispatched instantly.

SMOKE BOX   Cook your fresh fish in a smoke box, which can be purchased at most fishing stores. It gives fish a wonderful taste.

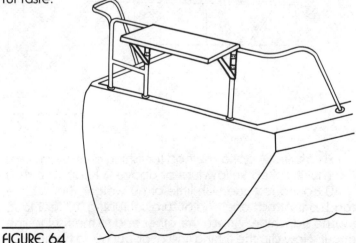

FIGURE 64

CLEANING BOARD   Screw a pair of angle irons to a board for cleaning fish. When needed, strap the board to the stern push-pit for an out-of-the-way station for cleaning fish (see Figure 64).

PLANKTON NET   There is the possibility that catching plankton will be of interest. Make a loop out of a wire clothes hanger and tape the waist of a pair of panty hose to the loop. Attach a three-line bridle to the wire, and let it out on a long line to drag slowly behind the boat.

CAMERA CARE   Of primary concern is protecting the camera and lens from salt and moisture. Using a lens filter and a metal lens cap and wiping the camera down after it has been out in the open will go a long way toward preventing corrosion.

Keep film in original containers, preferably in the icebox or the drink cooler.

When taking pictures on a rainy day, enclose the camera in a plastic bag, leaving only the lens exposed. Tape the bag tightly around the lens.

A few bags of silica gel, available at any camera store, will help to keep the camera dry in its case.

CAMERA TECHNIQUES   When using a camera at sea, consider these ideas for the harsh conditions you will encounter.

Try using a polarized filter that will capture deep colors and cut through the harsh glare of reflected light. Lens hoods will also help to cut glare. Consider shooting near sunset in order to get away from the too-bright sunlight of midday. Open the camera one to two stops if the subject is backlighted. Make a practice of bracketing when shooting in very strong sunlight. Using fast shutter speeds will generally be best under these conditions.

When using a long lens in rough seas, set shutter speeds at ⅟₂₅₀ to ⅟₅₀₀. Brace yourself and hold the camera loosely to get steady shots.

It is easier to get an accurate focus if the focus ring is turned quickly.

CAMCORDERS
The relatively new camcorders are a boon to cruising sailors. Recording your trip in sight and sound with a lightweight, battery-operated camcorder is a wonder most of us are still getting used to. Use it as a diary of the trip, or let the kids create a story for everyone's entertainment.

CUSTOMS DECLARATIONS
Whenever you leave territorial waters, it makes good sense to register all your cameras, electronic equipment, radios, and watches with U.S. customs. There can be no question when you return about where they were purchased.

UNUSUAL BON VOYAGE GIFTS
Cruising sailors always enjoy receiving small, useful gifts. Why not give a star identification book, nautical almanac, or cookbook. Stamps and stationery with the boat's name are always welcome. Spices, jams, jellies, chutney, and pickles make shipboard meals a treat.

Take along a blank book to be used by guests to record events during their visit on the boat.

NAUTICAL WRAPPING PAPER
Use old charts as clever gift wrapping paper for sailing friends.

GIFT CERTIFICATES
The next time a friend goes on a long cruise, give a telephone company gift certificate. He might get the hint and call you.

CANINE CONSIDERATIONS
If you travel overseas with a dog, be sure to check into each country's requirements for admission of a pet. At the very least they will require its vaccination records and health certificates. Think ahead and get prescription-strength worming and flea medicine from the veterinarian, who can also prescribe Panalog ointment for cuts, sores, and ear problems.

DRY PET WASH
It isn't easy to wash a pet while you are at sea. Try rubbing cornmeal or baking soda into its fur, then brushing it out well.

CAT MEDICINE   A sick cat on board is no fun at all. If your cat hates to take medicine, pour it on his fur and he will lick it off.

LITTER DEODORANT   Shredded newspaper and baking soda make adequate litter for an on-board cat.

LITTER LINERS   Cut up plastic garbage bags to make excellent litter box liners. Dispose of soiled litter by tying the ends of the liner with a twister and temporarily storing the bag in the towed dinghy.

REMOVING TAR FROM FUR   The only safe way to remove tar or paint from a pet's coat is to work white petroleum jelly into the fur and comb out the combined mess. Don't use paint remover or turpentine because these are quite toxic to animals.

NONMOVABLE FEAST   Place a piece of foam rubber under the cat or dog feeding dish to keep it from sliding or being pushed around the cabin floor.

SWIM TO BE CLEAN   Run a hose from the fresh-water system to the swim ladder. A quick fresh-water rinse after a salt-water bath will leave you fresh as a daisy. Much less water will be used compared to showering below.

SWIM LADDERS   One of the least effective sailboat accessories is the portable swim ladder. Consider installing a stainless steel folding stern ladder that can double as a gangplank.

WHALES AWAY   If playful whales are getting too close to the boat and causing some concern, frighten them off by banging on the hull or turning up the radio.

RELIEF IS SPELLED S-H-O-R-E

Most cruising sailors look forward to regular trips to shore. Even a task such as replenishing supplies is anticipated with a pleasure not normally felt at the hometown supermarket. These trips are well-earned relief away from the confinement of shipboard life. So, proudly disheveled and with a rocky gait, you make your way through town feeling very different from the land-locked passerby. Later, well refreshed, you return to your boat, the envy of those left behind.

SHORESIDE ACTIVITIES

Break up the sailing trip with frequent visits to seaside restaurants, historical sights, hikes with the kids, and shopping sprees for supplies. Ice cream cones never taste quite as delicious as they do when you have been at sea for a while.

FOLDING BICYCLES AND MOPEDS

Transportation on shore is a very real problem for sailors. Collapsible bicycles and mopeds are finally gaining popularity as a result of their lowered cost and excellent utility. Some mopeds weigh as little as 60 pounds and store folded into a waterproof bag of about 3-by-2-by-1 feet.

Bicycles weigh much less than mopeds, of course, and when they are collapsed they are easily stored in a lazaret or car trunk. Routine maintenance is limited to wiping down frequently with fresh water, keeping moving parts well greased and using petroleum jelly on corrodible parts.

SHELL COLLECTING

Collecting shells where permitted is a very rewarding hobby. Use good protective clothing such as rubber shoes, rubber gloves, a knife to pry shells loose, and a face mask to look beneath the surface. Loop a net bag over your wrist to carry your collection, and search the shoreline at low tide. After a thorough cleaning, wash shells with fresh water, and coat them with a thin film of oil to show their true colors.

SNORKELING EQUIPMENT

Snorkeling safety and comfort improve measurably when you wear an inexpensive pair of rubber-coated work gloves to protect hands from coral and sea urchins.

Full-footed fins are probably best because they are flexible, light, and fairly easy to walk in. Sneakers are heavy in the water, so consider using scuba diving neoprene boots to give protection to your feet. Consider buying translucent face masks that don't deteriorate as quickly as black masks. To remove the silicone release agent from a new mask easily, rub some toothpaste on the glass and rinse in fresh water. The normal lens of a snorkeling mask can be replaced with a prescription lens by a good dive shop. This may open up a whole new undersea world for some people. Choose a straight snorkel tube, not the curved type used by scuba divers.

SNORKELING TIPS To get water out of your mask, press on its brow, tilt your head back, and blow through your nose.

Put a coating of Vaseline on your moustache if you have trouble getting a good seal.

HAVING FUN WITH CHILDREN ON BOARD

Although there have been some attempts to write about children on sailboats, this is still one of the less commonly addressed subjects in sailing literature. Creating a happy, safe environment for children is a high priority for a cruising parent.

At all ages, children need independent activities, as well as intimate contact with the rest of the family. Toys, games, and books from home usually consume too much space for normal sailing craft. Therefore, using the boat's equipment to amuse and educate children reduces the clutter while providing unique shipboard entertainment. Running string about like cobwebs, shinnying up the mast support, building caves in the V-berth, reading, listening to tapes, fishing, and crabbing are just some of the many fascinating activities for children. The reward is a child who is not bored and who is eager to go sailing again.

INFANT CARRIER While in the cabin, you can carry an infant in the front carrying pouch that you use on shore. This leaves both hands free to steady yourself or to get some jobs done.

Select a secure place in the cabin where your child can be strapped down in a car seat. The body harness and cushioned chair provide excellent security for a baby.

DIAPER SERVICE   Put soiled cloth diapers in a net bag and tow them behind the boat. Once they are clean, rinse them with softened fresh water and dry in the sun.

FLOORBOARD PLAYPEN   If everything is secure above, place a cushion on the cabin floorboards with a pillow at each end for a perfect infant playpen.

COOKING FOR AN INFANT   A food grinder can turn table food into excellent baby food.

Because formula and dry milk store so well, it pays to use them while you cruise with an infant. Keep hot water handy in a good thermos for mixing dry formula quickly. Avoid the need to sterilize bottles by using the disposable kind.

NONSLIP BABY   Babies are very slippery while they are being bathed. Putting them in a T-shirt gives you a better grip.

TINY BLANKET   Beach towels are the perfect size for an infant blanket.

TINY SHEET   Use a pillow case as a sheet for the bassinet mattress.

SUN PROTECTION   Keep infants out of direct sun as much as possible by clothing them in cotton pajamas and brimmed hats.

Remember that infants need extra liquids on hot days.

LIFE VEST REFLECTOR   Put strips of glass bead reflector tape on a toddler's life jacket as an additional safety measure.

LIFELINE NETTING   Almost everyone agrees that putting rope netting on the lifelines is a necessity if toddlers are on board. Be sure, however, that the netting is not so tight that children can climb on it.

V-BERTH NETTING   Put netting across the front of the V-berth to make a built-in play pen and add safety at bed time.

TODDLER PLAY   Can you imagine the fun a toddler can have with a bucket of soap suds in the cockpit? Or, even better, how about having a small blow-up swimming pool in the cockpit when you are at anchor?

BLOWING BUBBLES   Another great sport for toddlers on the boat is blowing bubbles. If you are moving rapidly, the wind will blow the bubbles for them. Try blowing smoke into the bubbles with a straw or shining a flashlight on them at night.

GLASS HOLDERS   Give your toddler a better grip on a drinking glass by slipping a wide rubber band over the glass.

GUM IN HAIR   Because of the lack of facilities on board, removing gum stuck in your child's hair becomes doubly difficult. Try the old trick of rubbing peanut butter in with the gum. It will now comb out easily.
    Try using nail polish remover if the gum is stuck to nonsensitive skin areas.

HIGH CHAIR SUBSTITUTE   A potty chair can be a good substitute for a high chair in the cabin. Strap it to the dinette seat or on the cabin floor in front of a makeshift table.

DETERGENT GUN   Kids love to use old detergent spray bottles as squirt guns.

BEACH TOYS   It is easy to rinse the sand off beach toys if you carry them in a net bag and rinse them before getting back on board.

FINGER PAINT   For easier cleanup, put a small amount of dishwasher detergent into finger paints before use.

HOMEMADE PLAYDOUGH   Make homemade Playdough by mixing two cups of flour, a cup of salt, and enough water to produce a putty-like consistency.

INSTANT PLAY HOUSE   Cut doors and windows into an old sheet, and drape it over the dinette for a perfect playhouse.

WADING POOL   If you put a small wading pool full of water on the dock, children can rinse their feet free of sand and dirt before stepping back on board.

CAMPING OUT ON DECK   When spending the night at anchor, older children can sleep comfortably on deck using bed-size pieces of foam. The foam rolls up nicely and can be stuffed anywhere out of the way when not in use.

STORY TIME   A good rainy day pastime is to cut words from magazines and paste them onto paper to create a letter to a friend.

PICK UP STICKS   Improvise a game of pick up sticks with a bundle of dry spaghetti.

PITCHING WASHERS   A handful of washers from dad's toolbox makes a good game of miniature horseshoes on a taut blanket in the V-berth.

VIDEO TAPE STORIES   Kids will amaze you with the complex stories they can create and record on the video camera or audio recorder. Let them tape the production during the afternoon for an evening performance.

BIRTHDAY PARTY   By planning ahead, the kids can decorate the entire boat with streamers, balloons, signs, and party favors for a family celebration.

CORRESPONDENCE SCHOOLS   When you plan to go on a long cruise, consider the excellent correspondence courses offered by the Calvert School of Baltimore, Maryland, or the Berkeley Extension Service, University of California, Berkeley, California.

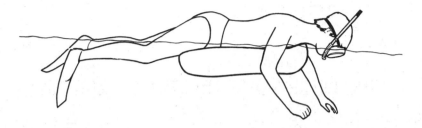

FIGURE 65

KIDS SNORKELING   When teaching snorkeling to children who know how to swim, improve their confidence by sending them out on a float. It will give inexperienced children support when they need a moment's rest (see Figure 65).

CHILDREN ON DECK   When nonswimming children are on deck, they should wear a life vest and a safety harness clipped to the boat. The lifeline should be long enough to reach the side but not long enough to go over.

TEACHING KIDS   It is hard not to be a demanding parent on board, but in the long run, more will be gained if you are not a perfectionist. Relieve the long hours on board by making frequent trips to shore.

Give older children real responsibilities. Let them operate the boat for a specific time with you as the crew.

Children often find it interesting to have a special piece of equipment assigned as their responsibility. Let them monitor the depth sounder or spiral coil the lines.

School-age children can be taught to steer to a landmark, sail the dinghy on a tether, gather headsails, help raise the main and coil lines. When the kids are really interested, let them run a man-overboard drill, steer by using compass bearings from the chart, start and stop the engine, trim the sail, and make calls on the radio.

You may not have children, but there are bound to be times when children and their parents come aboard as guests. Keep a small ditty bag filled with a variety of toys and books.

The parents can relax and sail while the children explore the bag of fascinating new toys.

THE DINGHY: SATELLITE TRANSPORTATION

A sailing dinghy or an inflatable raft with a small outboard extends your cruising range enormously. No longer confined to the boat, kids can row about on a tether, learn how to sail, or run errands. For the older children, learning how to stow the dinghy, tie it to shore, anchor it, protect and care for it become pleasant chores. For the adults, this secondary means of travel gives pleasure far beyond its humble appearance.

DECK THE DINGHY   Use two people, one on the main halyard, the other to position the dinghy, to simplify hoisting and placing it on deck.

STOWING ON DECK   It is preferable to stow a dinghy on deck upside down. Ease the difficulty of turning it upside down by using a special rig. Tie a rope bridle on a whisker pole. Then attach the bow painter to one end of the whisker pole and a line from the center of the dinghy's stern to the other end. With the bridle suspended by the main halyard, it is quite

FIGURE 66

easy to flip the dinghy over and lower it to its place on deck (see Figure 66).

DINGHY HANDLES
Two people can easily pick up a dinghy if four rope handles are put through the dinghy seats. Drill two holes for each handle and knot the rope underneath the seats. The handles also make good points to tie a bridle for winching the dinghy on board.

DINGHY DRAINS
Put removable drains in the dinghy bottom to let the water out once the dinghy is on deck.

GUNWALE GUARDS
Most dinghys come with very unsatisfactory gunwale guards. Fabricate guards of your own from twisted Dacron line bolted to the gunwale. Or slip Dacron line inside clear plastic tubing and bolt in the same manner.

Split plastic hose and bolt it to the gunwale with self-tapping screws.

Try using strips of synthetic carpeting, folded and tacked to the gunwale.

A somewhat crude but effective guard can be fashioned by splitting bicycle tires and bolting them to the gunwale.

At the very least, bend and attach a plastic fender around the bow and the outer ends of the stern.

TRANSOM GUARD
If you use the dinghy to kedge with an anchor on a chain, the chances are that the transom will get badly chewed up from the running chain. Fabricate a piece of galvanized sheet metal in a U-shape that will fit on the transom to protect it where the chain goes over.

SCULLING NOTCH
Put a sculling notch in the transom of the dinghy for the inevitable time when you have lost an oar. Place the remaining oar in the notch and with a back and forth sweeping motion the boat can be rowed with a single oar.

TOWING EYES
A towing eye placed low in the bow of the dinghy will make the dinghy tow better and prevent the painter from chafing the bow when at anchor.

A stainless steel D-ring mounted on a fabric pad can be glued on the bow of an inflatable raft as a towing eye.

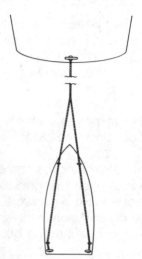

FIGURE 67

BIG RIGID DINGHY   Getting a big rigid dinghy to tow well is very difficult. Put a large U-bolt on the port side near the dinghy transom and another on the same side near the bow. Repeat this on the starboard side. Lead lines from the stern U-bolts, through the bow U-bolts, to the sailboat for smooth towing (see Figure 67).

TILLER EXTENSION   The dinghy trims better if you sit in the center and steer using an outboard tiller extension. A 2- to 3-foot length of PVC pipe sized to slip snugly over the tiller handle does the job well.

OUTBOARD FRESHWATER FLUSH   It is a good practice to regularly flush the outboard with fresh water. Rest the propeller in a plastic garbage pail filled with fresh water. Run the outboard long enough for a good flush.

OUTBOARD FUEL CONTAINERS   A quart squeeze bottle of fuel strapped under the seat makes it easy to refill the outboard without gasoline spills, even in rough water. Be sure that regulation markings are on the bottle to indicate its contents.

EXTRA FLOTATION   Because a swamped rigid dinghy will generally sink to its gunwales, installing extra flotation is a good idea. Place blocks of foam or foam fenders under the seats, which gives enough flotation to allow you to bail from inside. The extra fenders can be used at other times as gunwale guards.

DINGHY BAG   The dinghy anchor and rode can be kept in a canvas duffel bag stowed beneath a midship seat.

When you go offshore, secure a small bag of survival gear inside the dinghy.

TWO-PART DINGHY   One answer to the problem of having a dinghy that is large enough for the whole crew yet easy to stow on deck is the two-part dinghy. With the bow section nested in the stern section, it stows easily and can be assembled in a minute.

DINGHY DODGER   By gluing a piece of canvas over the bow of the inflatable dinghy, you can create an awning to provide a protected storage area.

CLEAN BOTTOM   To clean the bottom of the inflatable dinghy, wash with a strong solution of bleach and water. After rinsing, put on a good quality wax or renew with a brushable neoprene coating.

DINGHY FENDER   It may seem evident, but there will be a great deal less wear and tear on the inflatable if you carry a small foam fender to hold it off the dock and rocks.

SPARE VALVE AND PRESSURE GAUGE   Tape a spare valve under the inflatable's seat for the time when you need it.

The hot sun can lead to overinflation of the inflatable dinghy if it is not checked. Keep a pressure gauge on board for regular checks.

PUNCTUREPROOF THE BOTTOM   The bottom of the inflatable dinghy gets extra hard wear, so put a second layer of repair canvas on the inside where your feet and cargo poke about. Also add sacrificial fabric to the outside at the stern and the bow to protect against scraping each time the dinghy is bleached.

BOW HANDHOLD   Rubber handholds can be glued to the bow inside the inflatable. A passenger facing forward in the front seat can now have a secure hold when the dinghy is racing along using the outboard.

PROPER OARS   It is nearly impossible to row a dinghy with oars of improper length. To make the task as easy as possible, have oars that are twice the length of the dinghy's beam.

LOST OARLOCK   A temporary replacement for a lost oarlock is to loop the painter through the oarlock holder and hold it firm with your foot. This improvised oarlock will help you to row back to ship or shore.

ROWING THE DINGHY   Rowing an inflatable dinghy with a strong tide or current will make it difficult to reach your objective. Turn the dinghy bow into the wind or current and back slowly to your target with complete control.

DINGHY SAILING   Dinghy sailing, particularly for children, instills the instinct for sailing that is difficult to achieve on a big boat where weight and size reduce the "natural" feel. In a short period, a sailing dinghy can go through all the points of sailing that would take hours to experience on a large craft. Sail a dinghy again and get back to basics.

USES FOR THE SAILING DINGHY   Use the sailing dinghy to explore shallow waters and creeks, to teach children the points of sailing in a nonthreatening atmosphere, to take an anchor off for kedging, and, last of all, as satellite transportation.

INDEX